5

Understanding Elections

What's Your VOTE?

Author

Torrey Maloof

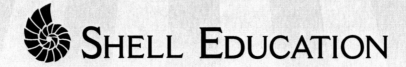
SHELL EDUCATION

Standards

To view how this information meets national and state standards, scan the QR code or visit our website at http://www.shelleducation.com and follow the on-screen instructions.

Publishing Credits

Corinne Burton, M.A.Ed., *President*; Emily R. Smith, M.A.Ed., *Content Director*; James D. Anderson, M.S.Ed., *Editor*; Grace Alba Le, *Multimedia Designer*; Stephanie Bernard, *Assistant Editor*; Don Tran, *Production Artist*

Image Credits

p. 15, LOC [LC-DIG-ppmsca-19870]; p.21, National Archives; p.26, Franklin D. Roosevelt Presidential Library and Museum; p.37, LOC [HABS DC,WASH,134--188], LOC [HABS DC,WASH,134--306], LOC [HABS DC,WASH,134--530], LOC [LC-DIG-ppmsca-16899]; p.39, LOC [LC-USZ62-25600]; p.39, National Archives; p.40, LOC [LC-USZ62-117121], LOC [LC-DIG-ppbd-00371], LOC [LC-DIG-ppmsca-19305], LOC [LC-USZ62-13028], LOC [LC-USZ62-138226], The Granger Collection, New York; p.48, LOC [LC-DIG-ppmsca-25556]; p.51, LOC [LC-USZ62-107700], LOC [LC-USZ62-117121], NASA, LOC [LC-USZ62-13040], LOC [LC-DIG-ppmsca-19305], LOC [LC-DIG-ppmsca-36075]; p.59, LOC [LC-DIG-ppmsca-08486], LOC [LC-DIG-ppmsca-08489]; p.70, LOC [LC-DIG-ppmsca-02929]; p.81, LOC [LC-USZC2-5233]; p.92, LOC [LC-DIG-ppmsca-19168]; p.103, Edited from Wikimedia Commons; p.114, LOC [LC-USA7-16837]; p.116, LOC [LC-USZ62-134651], LOC [LC-USZ62-126332], LOC [LC-USZC4-7730], LOC [LC-USZC4-7724]; Border Image, nick73/iStockphoto; Layout Elements, edge69/iStockphoto, sgursozlu/iStockphoto, marigold_88/iStockphoto, Yuri_Arcurs/iStockphoto; Illustrations, Timothy J. Bradley/Monique Dominguez/Evan Ferrell/Travis Hanson/Shutterstock; all other images iStockphoto & Shutterstock

Standards

© 2004 Mid-continent Research for Education and Learning (McREL)

© Copyright 2010. National Governors Association Center for Best Practices and Council of Chief State School Officers. All rights reserved.

Shell Education
5301 Oceanus Drive
Huntington Beach, CA 92649-1030
http://www.shelleducation.com
ISBN 978-1-4258-1353-6
© 2015 Shell Education Publishing, Inc.

★★★ **Table of Contents** ★★★

★★★ The Importance of Civic Education ★★★

★ ★ ★ ★ ★ ★ ★ ★ ★ ★ ★ ★ ★ ★ ★ ★ ★ ★

> "Young people must learn how to participate in a democracy."
> —*Constitutional Rights Foundation* 2000

It is the responsibility of those living in the United States to understand how civics relates to them. By being able to participate in a democracy, citizens can affect the nation and its well-being. Therefore, it is necessary for students to learn and understand civics. The National Council for the Social Studies (2010) states that social studies curricula should include opportunities to study "the ideals, principles, and practices of citizenship in a democratic republic." By learning civics, students can be committed to addressing social and government issues in a constructive way. However, in order to do this, students must understand the country and communities in which they live.

According to the National Standards for Civics and Government (Center for Civic Education 2014), the following are the organizing questions around which civic education should be based:

I. What is government and what should it do?

II. What are the basic values and principles of American democracy?

III. How does the government established by the Constitution embody the purposes, values, and principles of American democracy?

IV. What is the relationship of the United States to other nations and to world affairs?

V. What are the roles of the citizen in American democracy?

Teachers need to help students understand and respond to these civic questions so that students can apply their knowledge later in life when responding to daily events as adults in a democracy. Experiences during the K–12 school years lay the foundation for students to be able to evaluate situations and defend positions on public issues as well as influence civic life through working and managing conflict (Constitutional Rights Foundation 2000).

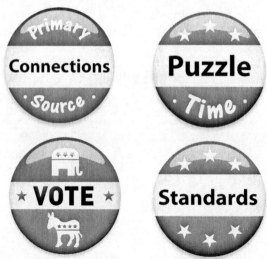

★ ★ ★ The Importance of Civic Education *(cont.)* ★ ★ ★

The lessons in this book bring about the following benefits and skills:

- increased written and oral communication

- working knowledge of government and democracy

- interest in current events

- higher likelihood of consistent voting and voting on issues rather than personality when an adult

- increased ability to clearly articulate opinions

- tolerance of differing opinions

- knowledge of how to make decisions even when others do not agree

- increased political and civic activeness

- appreciation of the importance and complexity of government

- increased civic attitude (Carnegie Corporation 2003)

In order for teachers to be effective, civic education needs to be recognized as a key aspect of today's curriculum. All of the aforementioned skills contribute to the goal of becoming a well-rounded, contributing, responsible, and civic-minded member of society outside of the classroom. However, these skills take time to develop and need to be integrated into the curriculum beginning in kindergarten and extending through 12th grade to be ultimately effective (Quigley 2005). Research suggests that children start to develop social responsibility and interest in politics before the age of nine. The way students are taught about social issues, ethics, and institutions in elementary school matters a great deal for their civic development (Kirlin 2005). Therefore, teachers have a responsibility to students to provide them with the activities necessary to learn these skills throughout their education.

★ ★ ★ ★ ★ ★ ★ ★

> "[C]hildren start to develop social responsibility and interest in politics before the age of nine."

Civic education can be taught both formally and informally. Intentional formal lessons imbedded in the curriculum give students a clear understanding of government and politics and the historical context for those ideas. This instruction should avoid teaching rote facts and give as much real-life context as possible. Informal curriculum refers to how teachers, staff, and the school climate can lead by example and illustrate to students how a working civic community operates (Quigley 2005). When adult role models portray and promote responsible civic engagement, students have a greater conceptual understanding of the formal, civic-based curriculum and how it relates to everyday life.

★ ★ ★ **How to Use This Book** ★ ★ ★

Overarching Themes

The lessons in this book cover three overarching themes, or units, that take students through the election process.

- **What Is a Presidential Election?**—This unit lays the foundation for elections. Students will make connections between rules and laws, learn about leadership, the importance of voting, and the characteristics of political parties.

- **Elect Me!**—In this unit, students will learn about the road to election day, characteristics of good leaders, and the responsibilities of leadership from national conventions to campaigning.

- **And the Winner Is...**—Students will experience the voting process and will learn about ballot counting and Inauguration Day in this unit.

Activities in this Book

The lessons in this book are divided into three sections. Each section is designed to engage student interest and enhance student knowledge of the lesson topic.

Paired-Texts Reading and Activities

Using paired fiction and nonfiction texts can be an engaging way to introduce a topic to students and allow them to compare and contrast various types of text. By pairing the texts, a connection is created between the content of both. Students may gravitate in interest toward one type of text—fiction or nonfiction. Presenting similar information in both types of text allows one passage to help build background knowledge while the other passage focuses on reinforcing that knowledge and building interest. Students will use graphic organizers to arrange their thoughts and participate in active learning opportunities with their peers.

Primary Source Connection

Using primary sources gives a unique view of history that other ways of teaching history are unable to do. Primary sources include newspaper articles, diaries, letters, drawings, photographs, maps, government documents, and other items created by people who experienced past events firsthand. Primary sources show students the subjective side of history, as many authors that experienced the same event often retell it in completely different ways. These resources also show students how events affected the lives of those who lived them. Primary sources make history real for students. As students view these historical items, they are then able to analyze the events from various points of view and biases. Each lesson contains a photograph or a document from election history.

★ ★ ★ **How to Use This Book** (cont.) ★ ★ ★

Activities in this Book (cont.)

Puzzle Time!

These are opportunities for students to practice content and problem-solving skills and to increase student engagement and interest in the lesson topic. Puzzles allow students to have fun while they reflect on what they have learned during the lesson. Students decode secret messages, use addition to create hidden images, find their way through fun mazes, and more!

Culminating Activity

This engaging activity is included to demonstrate students' overall knowledge of the election process and allow them to take part in a fun classroom election.

References Cited

Carnegie Corporation of New York and The Center for Information & Research on Civic Learning & Engagement. 2003. The Civic Mission of Schools. http://civicmission. s3.amazonaws.com/118/f7/1/172/2003_Civic_Mission_of_Schools_Report.pdf.

Center for Civic Education. 2014. National Standards for Civics and Government. http://www.civiced.org/standards.

Constitutional Rights Foundation. 2000. Fostering Civic Responsibility Through Service Learning. http://www.crf-usa.org/service-learning-network/8-1-fostering-civic-responsibility.html.

Kirlin, Mary. 2005. Promising Approaches for Strengthening Civic Education. White paper from the California Campaign for the Civic Mission of Schools http://www.cms-ca.org/CMS%20white%20paper%20final.pdf.

National Council for the Social Studies. 2010. *National Curriculum Standards for Social Studies*: A *Framework for Teaching, Learning, and Assessment*. Washington, D.C.: NCSS.

Quigley, C. N. 2005. The Civic Mission of the Schools: What Constitutes an Effective Civic Education? Paper presented at Education for Democracy: The Civic Mission of the Schools, Sacramento, CA. http://www.civiced.org/pdfs/sacramento0805.pdf

Presidential Elections

Standards

☑ Students know the fundamental principles of American democracy (e.g., the people are sovereign; the power of government is limited by law; people exercise their authority directly through voting; people exercise their authority indirectly through elected representatives).

☑ Students will analyze fiction and nonfiction texts and synthesize the information in a variety of ways.

Paired Texts Reading and Activities

★ **Every Four Years** (pages 10–11)— Have students read the story on page 10. Once they finish, ask students why Ripken's mom decided to vote for Arroz. Ask them why Ripken's mom thinks elections are important, citing examples from the text. Direct students to complete page 11 in small groups. Since they only have 30 seconds for their commercials, remind students to be creative, concise, and clear. Have groups perform their commercials for the class.

★ **Picking the President** (page 12)— Ask students to read the text on page 12. Have them number the different steps in the election process using colored pencils. Next, place the students in pairs to create infographics showing the election process steps. Share sample infographics to show a clear idea of what an infographic is. Students may need to conduct further research to make sure their infographics are informative.

★ **Steps to the Presidency** (page 13)—Have students use the informational text to help them list, in order, the steps in the election process. When students have finished, recreate the staircase on the board and go over the answers as a class. Finally, ask students where the best place on the staircase would be to place the "research step" that Ripken's mom completes in the text.

★ **Define, Refine, and Use** (page 14)—Students will use information from both the fictional story and the informational passage to define the three vocabulary words listed. Then, they will look up the words in dictionaries and refine their definitions. Finally, students will use each word in a sentence. After students have completed the assignment, have them share their responses with peers.

Presidential Elections *(cont.)*

Primary Source Connection

★ **Be Counted Primary Source** (pages 15–16)—Tell students to study the primary source on page 15. Read the background information as a class. Then, have students work independently to complete page 16. Point out that the posters they create should grab people's attention and make strong statements.

Puzzle Time!

★ **Election Cryptograms Vocabulary Puzzle** (page 17)—Students will enjoy figuring out the code to find the election related vocabulary words.

★ **Calculate and Color Elections Puzzle** (page 18)—Students will have fun figuring out which word is hidden in the puzzle full of math problems.

Answer Key

Steps to the Presidency (page 13)

> bottom step: primary elections
> second step: national conventions
> third step: presidential debates
> fourth step: Election Day
> top step: Inauguration Day

Define, Refine, and Use (page 14)

Student text-based definitions and sentences will vary. Dictionary definitions for the words are as follows:

> **election**—the process of choosing someone for a political office

> **candidate**—a person who runs in an election

> **vote**—to make an official choice in an election by casting a ballot

Election Cryptograms Vocabulary Puzzle (page 17)

1. debate
2. vote
3. polls
4. candidate
5. campaign
6. convention
7. inauguration

Calculate and Color Elections Puzzle (page 18)

answer: vote

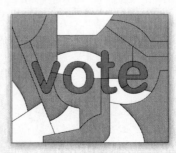

★ ★ ★ Every Four Years ★ ★ ★

"This is so stressful!" moaned Ripken.

"I know what you mean," sighed Ripken's mom. "I'm just not sure who to vote for."

Ripken looked at his mom in disbelief. "What in the world are you talking about, Mom? I'm talking about the game!"

"Oh, sorry, Sweetie. I'm just trying to figure out which candidate I should vote for in the election. It's in a few weeks, and I still haven't made my mind."

"How can you think about the election at a time like this? It's game 7 of the World Series®." Ripken's team was down by one run in the seventh inning. He couldn't believe his mom wasn't watching the game. After all, she was just as big a fan as he was. Instead, she was busy sifting through newspapers and magazines and reading articles on her laptop.

"Mom, I hope you are looking up what relief pitchers are left in our bullpen right now," grunted Ripken in response to his mom's furious typing.

"I think I'm going to vote for Arroz," declared his mom.

"You're only voting for her because she's a girl," retorted Ripken.

"Ripken Ryan Finley! That is not true. After all the research I have done, I believe she is the best candidate for the job. She shares my views on war, taxes, and helping those in need. She stands firm in her beliefs. She has many years of experience. She is wise and speaks well. I truly believe she cares for the safety and welfare of our country."

"Whatever you say, Mom. The game is back on!" Ripken replied, excitedly locking his eyes on the TV.

"Ripken, I don't think you understand the importance of the presidential election. It only happens every four years! Every four years, we the people pick the one person who will lead our country. Not every country gets to choose its leader."

"Mom! The game! Can we talk about this later?!" moaned Ripken.

"Ok, ok. But we will most definitely be talking about this later," Ripken's mom said sternly.

"Mom!" Ripken whined, taking his eyes momentarily off the TV.

"Let's go!" shouted his mom clapping her hands. Ripken laughed and turned his eyes back to the game just in time to see his favorite player hit a home run.

★ ★ ★ **Every Four Years** *(cont.)* ★ ★ ★

Directions: Imagine you have been given a 30-second commercial spot that will play during the World Series®. Follow the steps below to make a commercial to convince people to vote in the upcoming presidential election.

Step 1—Think It Through! Brainstorm different ideas. What will you say and do in the commercial? Be clever and creative!

Step 2—Plan It! Sketch below each part of your commercial and write notes on the lines.

Step 3—Practice! Perform your commercial a couple of times for practice. Memorize your lines. Speak loudly and clearly. Know where to stand and when to speak.

Step 4—Show Time! When you are ready, perform your commercial for the class.

★ ★ ★ Picking the President ★ ★ ★

People in the United States have political rights. This means they can take part in politics. Voting is one way to take part. Every four years, people head to the polls to vote for a new president. The president serves one term. That term lasts, you guessed it, four years! However, a president can run twice if he or she chooses to do so.

Elections are held on the Tuesday after the first Monday in November. Although Election Day is only one day, the election process is quite long. There are many steps in an election.

First, candidates announce that they will run in the election. When this happens, the official campaign has begun. There are two main political parties in the United States. A candidate is chosen to represent each party. This happens in primary elections. In the primaries, voters decide who they want to run for president. This person will represent their political party.

Next, the national conventions take place for each political party. They are like big meetings. The national conventions take place at the end of the summer. They last for many days. Songs are sung, and people share posters and signs.

The party platform, or policy, is stated. And the presidential candidate is appointed.

Now, it is time to hit the campaign trail. Candidates work hard to earn people's votes. They travel around the country. They meet with citizens, give speeches, join debates, make TV commercials, and do interviews. They also engage in debates.

In a debate, candidates strongly state their positions about issues. They try to convince voters that their ideas are better than the ideas of their opponents. The debates are shown on TV. Candidates can win many votes if they perform well in the debates.

Finally, it is November. Election Day is here! People go to the polls and cast their votes. They decide who they want the next president to be. The votes are counted, and the winner is announced. Sometimes the winner is announced on Election Day! But the new president does not start his or her new job on Election Day. The new president doesn't take office until Inauguration Day on January 20. This marks the end of the election cycle.

Directions: An infographic is similar to a chart or diagram, but it's more creative and visual! Infographics help people understand information quickly and easily. Summarize the steps in the election process in an infographic.

Name _____ Date _____

★ ★ ★ Steps to the Presidency ★ ★ ★

Directions: Using the steps of the election process listed in the box below, complete the graphic organizer. Write the steps in correct order, placing the final step at the top of the staircase. Use the information from *Picking the President* to help you.

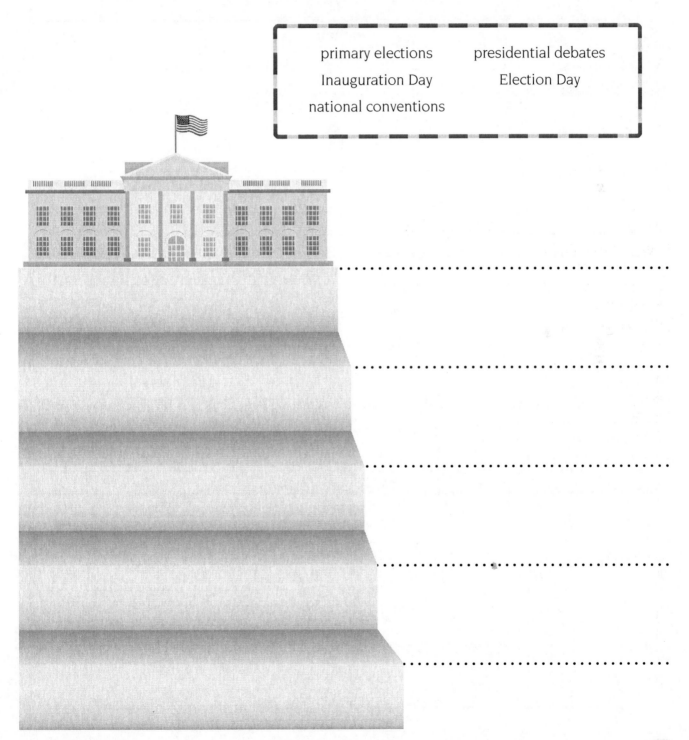

primary elections   presidential debates

Inauguration Day   Election Day

national conventions

★ ★ ★ Define, Refine, and Use ★ ★ ★

Directions: Use the information from both texts to write definitions for the words listed below. Next, look up the words in a dictionary and refine, or rewrite, your definitions to improve them and make them clearer. Then, use each word in a sentence.

election	
text-based definition	
dictionary definition	
sentence	

candidate	
text-based definition	
dictionary definition	
sentence	

vote	
text-based definition	
dictionary definition	
sentence	

★★★ **Be Counted Primary Source** ★★★

Primary Source Background Information

This poster is from the 1970s. It was created by the NAACP. That stands for the National Association for the Advancement of Colored People. The NAACP is a civil rights group. It helps minorities. In the 1960s and 70s it helped make sure that everyone had the right to vote. Back then, many minorities faced problems when they tried to vote. States would charge taxes to vote that minorities could not afford to pay. Or minorities would be forced to take tests that state officials knew they could not pass. Elections were not fair and equal. The Voting Rights Act was passed in 1965. It was improved in the 1970s. It made sure everyone had the right to vote. The NAACP wanted people to understand the importance of voting. They wanted minorities to know that everyone could make a difference if they voted.

National Association for the Advancement of Colored People, Library of Congress

★ ★ ★ **Be Counted Primary Source** *(cont.)* ★ ★ ★

Directions: Today, any citizen who is 18 years or older can vote. Ballots are even available in different languages to help keep elections fair for everyone. But many people still do not vote. Create a poster below that encourages people to get out and vote in the next presidential election.

★ ★ ★ Election Cryptograms Vocabulary Puzzle ★ ★ ★

Directions: In the puzzles below, each letter of the alphabet stands for another letter. You must break the code to solve the puzzles. Part of the code is given below to help get you started. Hint: All the answers are election–related vocabulary words.

F = A	Z = E	Q = I	Y = O	B = U
C = D	P = V	H = P	D = C	

1. Two or more people discuss issues during this.

___ ___ ___ **A** ___ ___
C   Z   R   F   X   Z

2. This is what you cast on Election Day.

___ ___ ___ ___
P   Y   X   Z

3. This is where you go to vote.

___ ___ ___ ___ ___
H   Y   W   W   J

4. This is a person who is running for political office.

___ **A** ___ ___ ___ ___ ___ **A** ___
D F G C Q C F X Z

5. Candidates have to work hard on this "trail" to get votes.

___ **A** ___ ___ **A** ___ ___ ___
D F K H F Q N G

6. A party's platform, or policy, is stated at this meeting that lasts for days.

___ ___ ___ ___ ___ ___ ___ ___ ___ ___
D Y G P Z G X Q Y G

7. This is the day the new president takes office.

___ ___ **A** ___ ___ ___ ___ ___ **A** ___ ___ ___ ___
Q G F B N B S F X Q Y G

Name _____   Date _____

★ ★ ★ Calculate and Color Elections Puzzle ★ ★ ★

Directions: Solve the problems below. Then, using the key below, color in the picture to find the answer to the question at the bottom.

Key

18 = red   24 = white   100 = blue

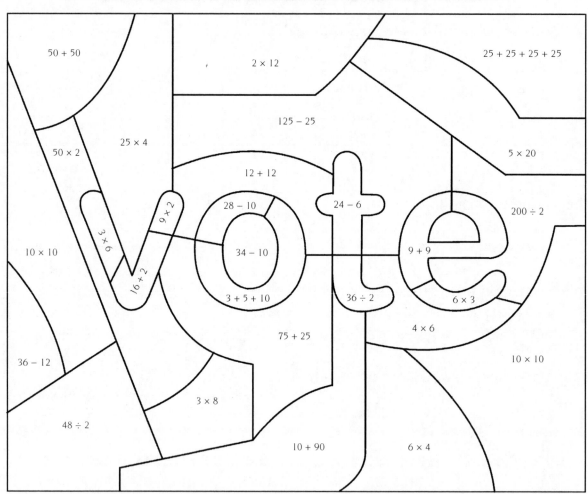

50 + 50

2 × 12

25 + 25 + 25 + 25

125 − 25

25 × 4

5 × 20

50 × 2

12 + 12

28 − 10   24 − 6

9 × 2

3 × 6

34 − 10   9 + 9   200 ÷ 2

10 × 10

16 + 2

3 + 5 + 10   36 ÷ 2   6 × 3

75 + 25   4 × 6

36 − 12   10 × 10

3 × 8

48 ÷ 2   10 + 90   6 × 4

Question: What do good citizens do on Election Day?

Answer

____   ____   ____

The U.S. Constitution

Paired Texts Reading and Activities

★ **It's in the Constitution!** (pages 21–22)—Tell students to read the poem on page 21. Then, read the poem together as a class. Have students pick their favorite stanzas and create illustrations for them. Select a few students to read the stanzas they chose and share their illustrations with the class. Next, direct students to complete page 22 independently using red and blue colored pencils. Go over the answers as a class.

★ **Election Laws** (page 23)— Have each student read the informational text on page 23 with a pencil in hand. Ask students to underline the laws listed in the text. Once they finish reading, go over as a class the reasons why laws are created. Then, guide students to discuss in pairs why they think election laws were created. Ask students to write new election laws or amend one of the laws that they do not agree with. Have students pair share their thoughts. Ask student volunteers to share their newly created or amended laws with the class.

★ **Presidential Requirements and Rules** (page 24)—Direct students to use information from both the poem and the informational passage to complete the graphic organizer. After students have completed the assignment, draw the graphic organizer on the board. Have students share their answers and write them on the board.

★ **I Think . . . Because . . .** (page 25)—With this activity, students will write their opinions on particular election laws. Before students begin this writing activity, discuss and review any opinion-writing strategies students have previously learned in class. When students are finished, ask volunteers to share their opinions with the class.

The U.S. Constitution *(cont.)*

Primary Source Connection

★ **Too Many Terms? Primary Source** (pages 26–27)—Study the primary source and read the background information on page 26 with students. Ask students to think about how they feel about the two-term limit on presidents. Consider providing some additional background information on President Franklin Delano Roosevelt. Tell students they need to have strong reasons to support their opinions. Then, have them complete page 27 independently. Ask students to share their opinions with two other students.

Puzzle Time!

★ **Election Laws Crossword Puzzle** (page 28)—Students will enjoy completing this crossword puzzle made from the vocabulary words for this lesson.

★ **Presidential Birthplaces Puzzle** (page 29)—Students will have fun finding out where presidents were born by using a code that is provided.

Answer Key

It's in the Constitution! (page 22)

Election laws are written in the Declaration of Independence. (F)	You must have been born in the United States to be the president. (T)
You must have lived in the United States for the last 14 years to be president. (T)	You have to be at least 34 to be president. (F)
You must be at least 21 years old to vote. (F)	Elections are a fair way to pick a president. (T)

False sentences rewritten to be true:

Election laws are written in the Constitution.
You have to be at least 35 to be president.
You must be at least 18 years old to vote.

Presidential Requirements and Rules (page 24)

Possible answers include the following: born in the United States; lived in the United States for the last 14 years; 35 years old or older; serves one four-year term; can serve another term if elected; can only be elected twice; & can serve for a maximum of 10 years.

Election Laws Crossword Puzzle (page 28)

Across
1. vice president
5. document
8. natural-born

Down
2. private
3. requirements
4. Constitution
6. term
7. resident

Presidential Birthplaces Puzzle (page 29)

1. Clinton   3. Nixon   5. Lincoln
2. Wilson   4. Truman

Bonus Answer: They all end with the letter *n*.

★★★ It's in the Constitution! ★★★

If the election rules are causing confusion,
look no further than the U.S. Constitution.
It lists the country's rules and laws,
which make elections fair for all.

If you are 18 years or older,
you can be a registered voter.
You can pick the president,
the next White House resident!

But to be the person in charge,
the list of rules is pretty large.
A local for 14 years or more,
Who's at least 35, not 34.
Being born in the U.S. is a must,
otherwise, your campaign will be a bust.

This is what our Constitution states,
it sure does help make our country great!
It clearly outlines what it takes
to vote or be the next Chief of State.

★ ★ ★ It's in the Constitution! *(cont.)* ★ ★ ★

Directions: Use the poem to help you label the statements below *true* or *false*. If a statement is true, color the box blue. If the statement is false, draw a red "X" on the box. At the bottom of the page, rewrite the false statements to be true.

Election laws are written in the Declaration of Independence.	You must have been born in the United States to be the president.
You must have lived in the United States for the last 14 years to be president.	You have to be at least 34 to be president.
You must be at least 21 years old to vote.	Elections are a fair way to pick a president.

_____

_____

_____

_____

_____

_____

_____

★ ★ ★ Election Laws ★ ★ ★

Are you allowed to run around in your classroom? Do your parents let you eat food in your bedroom? Are you allowed to ride a bike without a helmet? You have rules in your school, at home, and in your community. There are rules, or laws, for our country, too. They are written in the United States Constitution. This document lists the laws. It tells how our government works.

One law states when elections will be held. Elections for presidents are held every four years. Election Day is always the Tuesday after the first Monday in November.

Not everyone can run for president. First, you must be a natural-born citizen. This means that you were born in the United States. You must be at least 35 years old. Also, you must have been living in the United States for the past 14 years.

There are also laws for the vice president. The person running for president picks his or her vice president. If the president cannot serve for any reason, the vice president takes over. The vice president must meet all the same requirements as the president and must have lived in a different state from the president.

When the president is elected, there are more laws to follow. The president can serve two four-year terms. But that is it! You can only be president twice. However, a person can be president for 10 years, not just eight. How? Well some presidents take office in the middle of a term. This might happen if a president dies while in office or leaves for some reason. The new president can serve the remaining years in the current term and then may run for president for one or two more terms. Their years in office cannot be greater than ten years, though.

There are also laws for voting. In the past, not everyone could vote. Only white men over 21 could vote. Women, African Americans, American Indians, and other minorities could not vote. Changes were made to the Constitution. Now, every citizen 18 or older has the right to vote. You just have to register first! And you have the right to vote in private. This is why there are voting booths. No one can bully you or force you to vote for someone you do not want to. All these laws help keep elections fair, equal, and just for everyone.

Directions: If you had to write a new election law for the Constitution, what would it be? Or, if you could amend one of the laws, which one would it be and why? What would you change about it? Discuss your thoughts with a partner.

★ ★ ★ **Presidential Requirements and Rules** ★ ★ ★

Directions: Use the information from both texts to write details in the wheel about the requirements to be president.

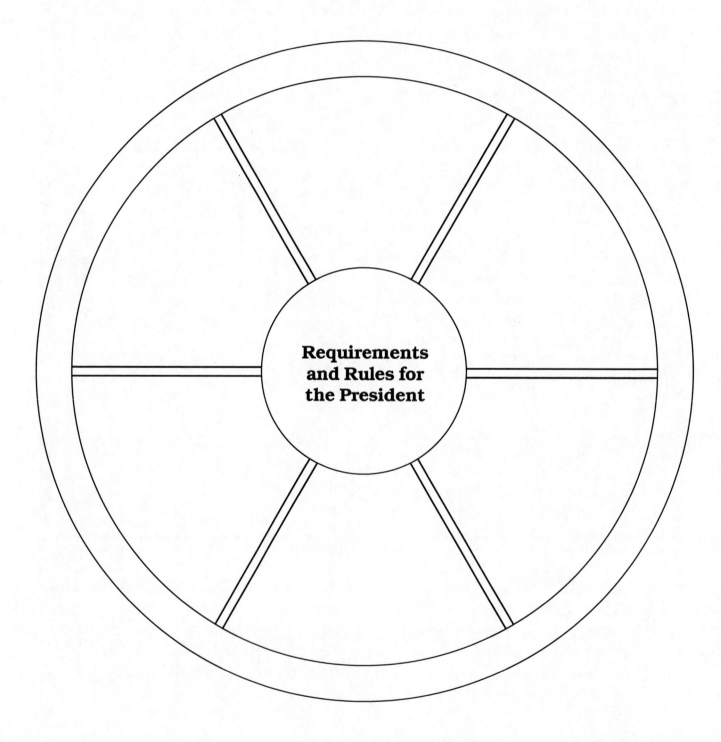

Requirements and Rules for the President

Name _____ Date _____

★ ★ ★ I Think...Because... ★ ★ ★

Directions: Complete the thought bubbles below by writing your opinions about certain election laws. Circle *fair* or *not fair* in each sentence. Then, be sure to provide a strong reason for each opinion.

I think the law that you have to be 35 to be president is **fair/not fair** because . . .

I think the law that you have to be 18 to vote is **fair/not fair** because . . .

I think the law that you have to be born in the United States to be president is **fair/not fair** because . . .

★ ★ ★ Too Many Terms? Primary Source ★ ★ ★

Primary Source Background Information

In 1940, Franklin Delano Roosevelt had already served two terms as president. He had been president for eight years. Back then, there was not a law that limited a president to two terms. So, in 1940, President Roosevelt ran for a third term, and he won! He went on to win a fourth term, too. Roosevelt was in office from 1933 to 1945. He led America during World War II. During his fourth term, he passed away. This campaign button was used by Republicans in 1940. Roosevelt was a Democrat. The Republicans did not think Roosevelt should run for a third term. In 1947, the 22nd Amendment was passed. It limited a president to two terms. Roosevelt was the only president to serve more than two terms.

Franklin D. Roosevelt Presidential Library and Museum

★ ★ ★ Too Many Terms? Primary Source *(cont.)* ★ ★ ★

Directions: Read the text in the box. Then, share your opinions in a paragraph. Be sure to include clear examples and reasons that support your opinions.

> President Franklin Delano Roosevelt helped lead America out of the Great Depression. He also helped win World War II. Many people consider him to be one of the best presidents in United States history. Other people believe that he should not have run for a third term. It was an "unwritten law" back then that presidents should only serve two terms. George Washington did not run for a third term. He said eight years was enough for any president. Was President Roosevelt right to run for a third term and a fourth term? For what reasons was it a good idea to pass a law that limits a president to two terms?

_____

_____

_____

_____

_____

_____

_____

_____

Name _____ Date _____

★ ★ ★ **Election Laws Crossword Puzzle** ★ ★ ★

Directions: Use the clues to complete the puzzle with the words given in the Word Bank.

Word Bank

Constitution	document	natural-born	private
requirements	resident	term	vice president

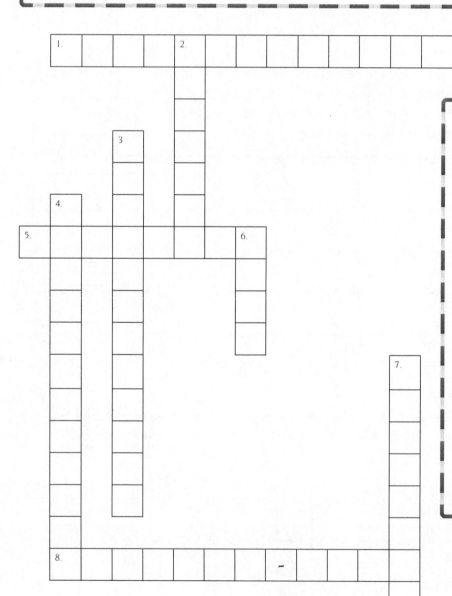

Across

1. ranks just below the president

5. an official paper

8. born in the United States

Down

2. not known by the public

3. necessities

4. the set of laws for our country

6. the length of time a person is in office

7. local inhabitant

★ ★ ★ Presidential Birthplaces Puzzle ★ ★ ★

Directions: To be president of the United States, you have to be born in the United States. Use the number chart to help you find out which presidents were born in the locations listed below.

1. Hope, Arkansas

___ ___ ___ ___ ___ ___ ___
3   12   9   14   20   15   14

2. Staunton, Virginia

___ ___ ___ ___ ___ ___
23   9   12   19   15   14

3. Yorba Linda, California

___ ___ ___ ___ ___
14   9   24   15   14

4. Lamar, Missouri

___ ___ ___ ___ ___ ___
20   18   21   13   1   14

5. Hodgenville, Kentucky

___ ___ ___ ___ ___ ___ ___
12   9   14   3   15   12   14

I = A	10 = J	19 = S
2 = B	11 = K	20 = T
3 = C	12 = L	21 = U
4 = D	13 = M	22 = V
5 = E	14 = N	23 = W
6 = F	15 = O	24 = X
7 = G	16 = P	25 = Y
8 = H	17 = Q	26 = Z
9 = I	18 = R	

Bonus Question: What do the last names of these presidents all have in common?

_____

_____

The Presidency

Standards

☑ Students know the major duties, powers, privileges, and limitations of a position of leadership (e.g., class president, mayor, state senator, tribal chairperson, president of the United States); and know how to evaluate the strengths and weaknesses of candidates in terms of the qualifications required for a particular leadership role.

☑ Students will analyze fiction and nonfiction texts and synthesize the information in a variety of ways.

Paired Texts Reading and Activities

★ **For the Greater Good** (pages 32–33)—Tell students to read the science fiction story on page 32. Discuss the characteristics of science fiction with the class. Take a class survey and ask students if they believe this story could have happened. Have students justify their responses. Then, direct students to individually complete page 33. Have volunteers share their drawings and dialogue with the class.

★ **One Tough Job** (page 34)— Have each student read the informational text on page 34 with a pencil in hand. Tell them to underline all the characteristics a president should have. Ask students to circle all the duties a president has. Once they finish reading, have students compile a list of 10 characteristics they think a president should have. Direct them to rank the list in order of importance. Then, have students share their lists with partners.

★ **Characteristics of a President** (page 35)—Have students use information from the informational passage to complete the graphic organizer on this page. Then, tell them to use the science fiction story to answer the text-dependent question at the bottom of the page. Go over student responses as a class.

★ **President Trading Cards** (page 36)—Before the class begins, write the names of the presidents on scraps of paper and throw them in a hat. If you would like, leave some of the lesser-known presidents out of the hat. Direct each student to pick a president out of the hat. Have students research their presidents using library books or the Internet and create trading cards for their presidents. Allow students time to swap trading cards to learn about different presidents and their characteristics.

The Presidency *(cont.)*

Primary Source Connection

★ **White House Primary Source** (pages 37–38)—Study the primary source and read the background information on page 37 with students. Ask if any students have ever visited the White House and ask them to share their experiences with the class. Have students complete page 38. Divide the class into groups to make short presentations of the changes they would make. Tell students to ask questions about each presentation. Explain that each presenter should answer at least one question about his or her presentation.

Puzzle Time!

★ **Vocabulary Picture Puzzle** (page 39)—Students will enjoy putting the puzzle pieces together to connect the pictures with the correct vocabulary words.

★ **Wartime Presidents Puzzle** (page 40)—Students will have fun connecting each president's picture to the war that took place during his presidential term(s).

Answer Key

Characteristics of a President (page 35)

President	Characteristic
George H.W. Bush	military experience
Jimmy Carter	good communication skills
Dwight D. Eisenhower	military experience
John F. Kennedy	good leadership skills
Abraham Lincoln	smart
Franklin D. Roosevelt	good at making decisions
George Washington	military experience

Students' answers on Eisenhower will vary but should have text evidence to support their opinions.

President Trading Cards (page 36)

Trading cards will vary but should include the names and pictures of the presidents, the years they were in office, and characteristics of the presidents.

Vocabulary Picture Puzzle (page 39)

communication goes with Roosevelt picture

amendment goes with 19th Amendment picture

experience goes with Eisenhower picture

nuclear war goes with explosion picture

peace treaty goes with Camp David Accords picture

Wartime Presidents Puzzle (page 40)

The War of 1812 = James Madison

The Civil War = Abraham Lincoln

World War I = Woodrow Wilson

World War II = Franklin D. Roosevelt

The Vietnam War = Lyndon B. Johnson

The War on Terror = George W. Bush

★ ★ ★ For the Greater Good ★ ★ ★

It was the middle of February 1954, and President Eisenhower was not happy. He should have been on vacation in Palm Springs. Instead, he was in New Mexico.

"I'm the president! What do you mean you can't tell me what this is all about?" barked the president as he entered the bunker at Holloman Air Force Base.

"I understand your frustration, Mr. President. You will learn soon enough what this is about," remarked John Dulles, the secretary of state. He led the president down a narrow staircase. With each step, the men descended deeper underground. The two men turned a corner to find 10 guards with large guns and two men in suits. One man was Charles E. Wilson, the secretary of defense. The other man was J. Edgar Hoover, the director of the FBI.

"Well if you two are here then this must be big," remarked the stunned president.

"We've had an incident, Mr. President," mumbled Wilson.

"That's what you're calling it?" huffed Hoover, rolling his eyes.

A heavy steel door with a "No Entry" sign was forcibly flung open by two of the guards. The four government leaders entered the poorly lit, damp room. There was a large steel table in the middle of the room with two people seated with their backs to the door. As the president walked past the table, he stopped abruptly.

"What are those?" asked the president in disbelief. He couldn't comprehend what he was looking at. They were not people. They were not human. What were they?

"Mr. President, these are extraterrestrial beings. They claim to be explorers from another world—a world in a distant galaxy," Wilson calmly stated.

It took the president quite some time to wrap his head around what was happening. He stood silent. He couldn't understand why everyone was acting so calm. For heaven's sake, there were aliens in the room! If the public found out, there would be mass chaos.

After days of discussion, the president and his men felt confident that the extraterrestrials were peaceful explorers who meant no harm. Intergalactic peace treaties were signed.

"The world does not need to know about any of this. The human race is not ready for such news. For the greater good, we must keep all this from the public," stated the president firmly. Everyone present agreed. The treaties and other files were sealed in a special folder labeled with an "X" and taken back to FBI headquarters.

Little did these four men know that in the next decade, the United States would be sending its own explorers into space. To this date, the seal on the X files has yet to be broken.

★ ★ ★ **For the Greater Good** *(cont.)* ★ ★ ★

Directions: Visualizing can help you better understand a story. Think about the story you read. What do you think the aliens look like? What do you think they say to the president? Draw a detailed picture in the box below. Then, write dialogue that shows the aliens' peaceful intentions.

_____

_____

_____

_____

_____

★ ★ ★ One Tough Job ★ ★ ★

Being president can be fun. You live in the White House. You have your own chef. You get to fly in your own airplane. And you get to be in charge of the entire country! But being president is also one tough job.

Presidents have to be good at making decisions. They make big choices that can change the whole world. President Franklin D. Roosevelt had to decide if America should join the fight in World War II. When America did enter the war, he made decisions that helped bring the war to an end.

Presidents also have to have great communication skills. They have to talk to leaders from other countries. President Jimmy Carter had to work with the leaders of Egypt and Israel. The two countries had been at war for years. Carter got the leaders to agree to a peace treaty.

Presidents must be smart. They have to know which laws to approve and reject. The Constitution lists the laws for the United States. Changes made to the Constitution are called amendments. President Abraham Lincoln signed the 13th Amendment, which made slavery illegal.

Presidents need to be good leaders. They not only lead our country, but also our military. They are in charge of the armed forces. They meet with military leaders and work to keep our country and the world safe. President John F. Kennedy had to meet with military leaders to find a way to avoid a nuclear war with the Soviet Union (now Russia).

Presidents must have a wide variety of experiences. It is a difficult and stressful job. Most people who become president have worked in the government. Many of them have good educations. Some presidents have military experience. President George H.W. Bush was a pilot in World War II. President Dwight D. Eisenhower was a general in that war, and he helped bring about victory and peace. President George Washington led the army during the American Revolution.

Not everyone is fit to be president. That is why voting is so vital. People need to vote for the person who will be the best leader for our country. They need to choose a president who will make choices that are in the best interest of our country and its citizens.

Directions: Make a top-10 list of characteristics you feel a candidate running for president should have. When you have finished your list, rate each characteristic on a scale of 1 to 10, with 10 being the most important. Compare your list with a partner.

★★★ Characteristics of a President ★★★

Directions: Use the information from the *One Tough Job* text to write characteristics of the presidents listed below. Then, answer the questions at the bottom of the page.

President	Characteristic
George H.W. Bush	
Jimmy Carter	
Dwight D. Eisenhower	
John F. Kennedy	
Abraham Lincoln	
Franklin D. Roosevelt	
George Washington	

In the science fiction text, why does President Eisenhower decide not to tell Americans about the alien visitors? Do you think he makes the right decision? Does this make him a good president? Why or why not? Use evidence from the text to support your answer.

_____

_____

_____

_____

Name _____ Date _____

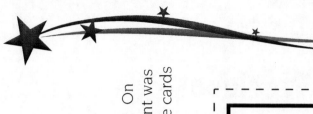

★ ★ ★ President Trading Cards ★ ★ ★

Directions: Research your president using books and the Internet. Then, create a trading card for your president. On the front of the card, write his name and draw a picture of the president. On the back, write the years the president was in office and list the president's strongest characteristics. Cut out the card and glue the two sides together. Trade cards with your classmates so that you can learn more about each president.

★ ★ ★ White House Primary Source ★ ★ ★

Primary Source Background Information

The White House is located at 1600 Pennsylvania Avenue in Washington, D.C. It is where the president lives and works. The White House has 132 rooms and 35 bathrooms. There are six floors, including a basement and a sub-basement. The house has eight staircases and three elevators. There is a huge kitchen and a staff that can make dinner for 140 guests. President Nixon built a bowling alley in the White House. President Ford installed an outdoor swimming pool. There is a jogging track and a putting green. There is a music room and a movie theater. There was a tennis court, but President Obama turned it into a basketball court. There is a beautiful rose garden and a large vegetable garden.

Jack E. Boucher, Frances Benjamin Johnston, Library of Congress

Name _____   Date _____

★ ★ ★ White House Primary Source (cont.) ★ ★ ★

Directions: Over time, presidents and their wives have changed the White House. Some have redecorated. Others have added things to it. Imagine you have just been elected president. What will you change about the White House? Sketch pictures below to illustrate your ideas. Then, write two sentences explaining your changes and why you think they will help you be a better leader.

_____

_____

_____

_____

★ ★ ★ Vocabulary Picture Puzzle ★ ★ ★

Directions: Read each sentence. Complete each sentence with a vocabulary word from the Word Bank. Which picture do you think best matches the vocabulary word in each sentence? Cut out the puzzle pieces and put together each picture with the correct sentence.

Word Bank

peace treaty   communication   amendment   nuclear war   experience

In 1920, President Wilson made an

_____

to the Constitution so that women could vote.

Some presidents, like Eisenhower, have

_____

being leaders in a war.

President Carter helped the leaders of Egypt and Israel sign a

_____.

President Kennedy helped stop a

_____

_____

that could have destroyed the world.

President Roosevelt used his

_____

skills when he met with leaders from other countries to help bring an end to World War II.

Name _____ Date _____

★ ★ ★ Wartime Presidents Puzzle ★ ★ ★

Directions: One of the hardest parts about being a president is leading the country during a war. These leaders had to do just that. Draw a line from each president to the war that was fought during his term. You may use the Internet to help you.

Lyndon B. Johnson

George W. Bush

The War of 1812

The Civil War

Franklin D. Roosevelt

World War I

World War II

Abraham Lincoln

The Vietnam War

James Madison

The War on Terror

Woodrow Wilson

Political Parties

Standards

☑ Students know how the values and principles of American democracy can be promoted through participating in government (e.g., voting, keeping informed about public issues, writing to legislators, serving on juries).

☑ Students will analyze fiction and nonfiction texts and synthesize the information in a variety of ways.

Paired Texts Reading and Activities

★ **Frenemies for No Reason** (pages 43–44)—Have students read the story on page 43. Then, go over the directions on page 44 as a class. Explain that their options can be fun or even impossible (for example, to solve a problem with their parents, they can offer to send them on vacation). Direct students to complete the page individually. Have volunteers share the solutions they chose to implement.

★ **Join the Party** (page 45)—Read the text on page 45 as a class. During the reading, have students circle the names of political parties and underline details that describe the parties using colored pencils. Then, hold a class discussion on the importance of staying informed on public issues. Explain why it is important to know what and who you are supporting when joining a political party. Place students in pairs to create posters with symbols and words to represent the political parties. (Note: Research may be needed to make sure their posters are informative.) Have students hang their posters in the classroom.

★ **Comparing Political Parties** (page 46)—Students will use information from both the fictional story and the informational passage to complete the Venn diagram and text-dependent question on this page. After students have completed the assignment, have them share their responses with peers.

★ **Making Your Own Platform** (page 47)—Before this activity begins, discuss the components of strong opinion writing as a class. Explain to students that they should state their opinions clearly, support their opinions with strong details, and include strong conclusions on their paragraphs. Go over the directions as a class, have students mark their opinions on page 47, and write their paragraphs.

Political Parties *(cont.)*

Primary Source Connection

★ **Political Parties Cartoon Primary Source**
(pages 48–49)—Study the primary source on page 48 with students. Have them read the background information in pairs. Go over page 49 as a class. Discuss possible interpretations of the political cartoon. Then, direct pairs of students to complete page 49. Encourage students to research the views of the political parties using the Internet or other resources.

Puzzle Time!

★ **Political Parties Vocabulary Search** (page 50)—Students will enjoy completing this puzzle that lists political parties through history.

★ **Presidents' Parties Puzzle** (page 51)—Students will have fun figuring out which presidents belonged to which parties using pictures and letter clues. To make this puzzle easier, give students access to a list of the presidents.

Answer Key

Comparing Political Parties (page 46)

Democratic Party: liberal; strong government; create opportunities for every person; support economic growth; affordable health care for all citizens; support social groups; donkey

Republican Party: conservative; careful about spending money; strength lies with people; people should be responsible for themselves; people should keep more of the money they earn; preserve national strength and pride; elephant

Both: have ideas about how government should work; keep our nation safe

Political Parties Vocabulary Search (page 50)

N					G		N			A	T
	A			R		A			N	L	S
		I		E		C		T		I	I
		R	E		I			I		B	L
		N	A	L			F			E	A
		B	T			E				R	R
		U		R	D					T	E
	P		F		E	E	G	I	H	W	Y	D
D	E	M	O	C	R	A	T	B			E
R			A		E			I			F
		L			E		L				
N	O	I	T	U	T	I	T	S	N	O	C
	S						O				
T								I			
									L		

Presidents' Parties Puzzle (page 51)

Democrat	Republican
Franklin Delano Roosevelt	Abraham Lincoln
John F. Kennedy	Theodore Roosevelt
Bill Clinton	Ronald Reagan

Bonus Answer: He did not belong to a political party. He stayed neutral.

★ ★ ★ Frenemies for No Reason ★ ★ ★

by Kiley Smith

Debbie and Jasmine came from two perfectly lovely families with two perfectly different worldviews. Debbie's parents were Republicans. Jasmine's parents were Democrats. This, although an adult matter, is what started the girls' feud. It created a wedge in their friendship.

"Why won't you just eat the sandwich?" said Jasmine to a very stubborn Debbie.

"It's burnt on the edges! I'm picky, okay?" Debbie huffed.

"You're so dorky," snapped an irritated Jasmine.

"I may be dorky, but at least I'm not a donkey!" Debbie retorted. Jasmine felt offended, but she recovered quickly.

"Oh, so we're talking about politics again? Well then, if I'm a donkey, you are a big, fat, stinky, elephant!"

The two friends continued to bicker, not noticing that another girl had sat down at their table. The girl interrupted Debbie and Jasmine with a loud cough.

Jasmine turned to the girl and said in a snarky manner, "Are you okay?"

Debbie stood up and sat next to the girl, pushing Jasmine out of the way. "Hi! I'm Debbie. What's your name?"

The girl replied politely, "My name is Katherine. And I think you two are wrong to bicker."

Jasmine and Debbie frowned, "What do you mean?" they both asked at the same time.

"What I mean is," Katherine began, "You girls are sixth graders. Why are you even worried about political parties? You should be able to be friends either way."

Debbie and Jasmine looked at each other. Katherine did have a point.

"Also, don't feel like you have to follow the same political party as your parents. You're free to make your own decisions in life," Katherine declared.

Debbie and Jasmine turned to each other and realized she was right. The two girls decided to go home and do some reading about political parties. They would then choose which party they wanted to support.

The next day, Debbie and Jasmine sat together on the bus.

"I decided which party I like best!" Jasmine sang.

"Me too!" Debbie declared. "Let's say it on three. One . . . Two . . . . Three!"

"Republican!" Jasmine shouted.

"Democrat!" Debbie exclaimed.

Name _____ Date _____

★ ★ ★ Frenemies for No Reason (cont.) ★ ★ ★

Directions: What are some of the issues you face each day? They might include how much homework you have, dealing with peer pressure, or finding time for extracurricular activities. List ten issues you face. Next, pick five issues and suggest solutions for them. Finally, pick your favorite solution and describe how you can put that solution in action.

10 Important Issues	5 Possible Solutions

★ ★ ★ ★ ★ ★ ★ ★ ★ ★ ★ **Take Action!** ★ ★ ★ ★ ★ ★ ★ ★ ★ ★

_____

_____

_____

_____

_____

★ ★ ★ Join the Party ★ ★ ★

Political parties first began in 1796. Our country was new. The government had just started. People joined these parties. They had ideas about how the government should work. They joined other people who had the same ideas.

The first two parties were the Federalists and the Anti-Federalists. The Federalists believed in a strong national government. The Anti-Federalists did not want a strong national government. They wanted each state to run itself.

Party names and ideas have changed over the years. Today, we have two major parties. They are the Democratic and Republican parties.

The Democratic Party is said to be *liberal*. This means that they are open to new ideas and ways of behaving that are not traditional. They also believe in a strong government. Their website says that the party wants to keep our nation safe. They want to create opportunities for every person. They support strong economic growth. They want affordable health care for all citizens. Democrats support social

groups. They want the government to provide services for the people. Their symbol is the donkey.

The Republican Party started in 1854. Republicans are said to be *conservative*. This means that they believe in the traditional practices in society. Their website tells what they believe. They believe that the strength of our country lies with the people. They believe that people should be responsible for themselves. They also believe that the government should be careful with its money, and people should be able to keep more of the money they earn. They think the government should only give services that cannot be done by the people. They say that we should value and preserve our national strength and pride. Their symbol is the elephant.

There are a lot of smaller parties, too. These "third parties" have ideas that are important to a lot of people. Third parties give citizens more choices. This is helpful for people who do not agree with the two main political parties.

Directions: Choose one of the two main political parties. Create a poster that shows symbols and words that represent that political party. Conduct further research as necessary to make sure your poster is informative. Be sure to include images and visuals to support your details.

★ ★ ★ Comparing Political Parties ★ ★ ★

Directions: Use the information from *Join the Party* on page 45 to compare the Democratic Party to the Republican Party. Then, answer the question below.

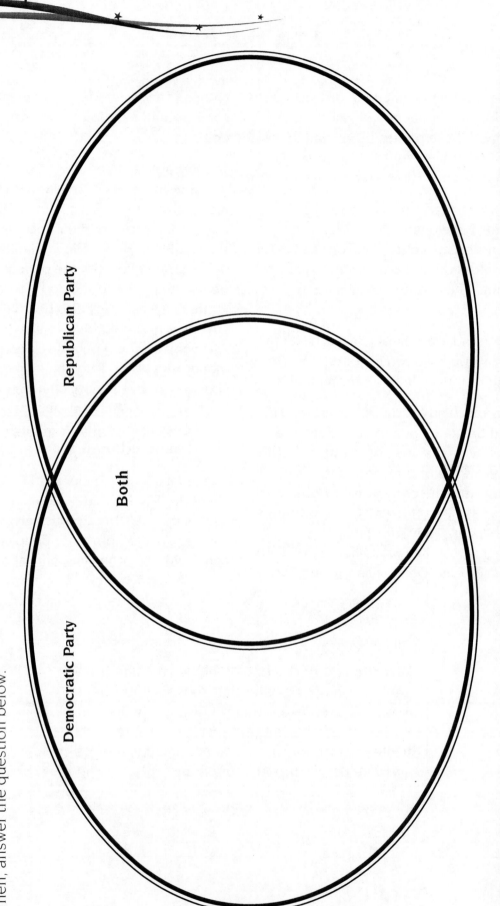

Republican Party

Both

Democratic Party

In what ways did the differences listed in your Venn diagram affect the friendship between Debbie and Jasmine? Write your answer on the back of this page. Use examples from *Frenemies for No Reason* to support your answer.

★ ★ ★ Making Your Own Platform ★ ★ ★

Directions: Below are differing viewpoints about today's important issues. Put a check in the box on each row that matches your own viewpoint. Then, on a separate sheet of paper, write a paragraph describing your own political opinion on one of the issues.

Issue	View One	View Two
Government	The government should provide services to the people.	The government should encourage people and businesses to provide services to the people.
Security/ Defense	Opposes nuclear buildup in the United States. Believes that peace is achieved through worldwide relationship building.	Believes in a proactive military and defense. Supports building weapons and technology that serve to protect our nation. Believes that peace is achieved through strong defense.
Tax Reform	Supports tax cuts. Saves money by cutting government programs.	Uses taxes to fund programs and services for the people.
Education	Opposes vouchers. Enacts new taxes to decrease class size and hire new teachers.	Promotes school choice and the use of vouchers.
Energy	Supports tax incentives for energy production. Believes that all sources of energy should be developed, including oil.	Wants to find renewable energy sources and solutions. Opposes increased drilling, especially in the United States.

★ ★ ★ Political Parties Cartoon Primary Source ★ ★ ★

Primary Source Background Information

This is a political cartoon from 1901. It is titled "A Political Game." It shows two women leaning out windows. The woman on the left is dressed in old and tattered clothes and does not look wealthy. She represents the Democratic Party. The older woman on the right is well dressed and looks wealthy. She represents the Republican Party. The balance scale between them represents party politics. Rear Admiral Winfield S. Schley is on the left. He is trying to upset the balance by pulling on the chains. This causes the scale to swing wildly. Admiral William T. Sampson is on the right. He is trying to hang on.

Udo J. Keppler, Library of Congress

Name _____ Date _____

★ ★ ★ Political Parties Cartoon Primary Source *(cont.)* ★ ★ ★

Directions: How do you think the cartoon on page 48 applies to today's political parties? Think about one issue the two parties disagree over today. In the space below, write and draw what each party might believe about this issue.

Issue: _____

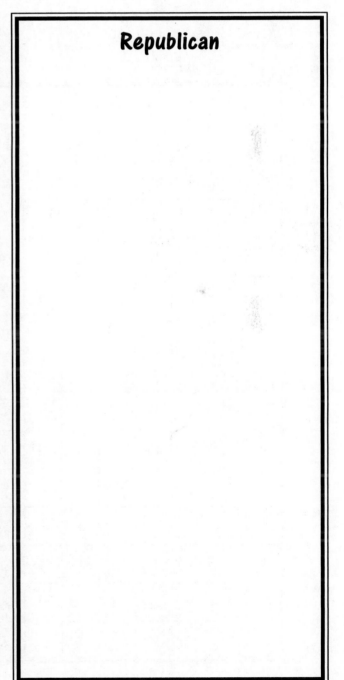

Democrat	Republican

Name _____ Date _____

★★★ Political Parties Vocabulary Search ★★★

Directions: Find these political parties from throughout American history in the word search puzzle.

Anti Federalist	Free Soil	Liberty	Constitution	Green
Democrat	Libertarian	Whig	Federalist	Republican

N	X	X	D	H	C	U	G	M	N	M	Y	B	A	T
P	A	W	D	Y	R	R	N	A	U	O	R	N	L	S
K	O	I	A	D	E	V	C	H	H	E	T	B	I	I
M	B	Z	R	E	P	I	L	U	E	I	E	K	B	L
C	W	L	N	A	L	Y	O	M	F	S	T	K	E	A
J	Y	O	U	B	T	E	A	E	H	C	T	E	R	R
R	R	D	U	X	T	R	D	Q	C	A	Y	Z	T	E
L	Q	P	F	F	F	E	E	G	I	H	W	D	Y	D
D	E	M	O	C	R	A	T	B	Y	N	Q	A	Y	E
R	O	M	O	A	J	E	T	A	I	A	Y	G	X	F
O	B	Q	L	T	H	K	E	M	E	L	L	X	I	V
N	O	I	T	U	T	I	T	S	N	O	C	C	F	W
W	S	Y	B	O	N	J	B	A	O	Y	U	T	G	O
T	H	U	U	D	H	P	A	T	V	I	Z	A	M	T
G	L	O	H	L	W	X	Z	T	Z	M	L	Q	O	M

Name _____ Date _____

★ ★ ★ Presidents' Parties Puzzle ★ ★ ★

Directions: Which parties did these famous presidents belong to? Use the pictures and the letters to help you fill in each president's name.

Democratic Party

_ r a n _ l i n   _ o _ n _.   B i _ _
_ e l a n o   _ e _ _ e d y   C _ _ _ t o n
_ o o s e v e _ t

Republican Party

_ _ _ _ _ h a m   T h e o _ _ _ _ _   _ o _ a l d
_ _ _ c o l n   R _ _ s e _ _ _ _ _   _ e a g a _

Bonus Question: Which party did George Washington belong to? Use books and the Internet to help you find the answer.

_____

The National Convention

Standards

☑ Students know the fundamental principles of American democracy (e.g., the people are sovereign; the power of government is limited by law; people exercise their authority directly through voting; people exercise their authority indirectly through elected representatives).

☑ Students will analyze fiction and nonfiction texts and synthesize the information in a variety of ways.

Paired Texts Reading and Activities

★ **Covering the Convention** (pages 54–55)—Place students into groups of three to read the reader's theater script on page 54. Then, ask for three volunteers to read it in front of the class. Have students complete page 55 individually or in pairs. Encourage them to ask questions that cannot be answered with a *yes* or *no*. Ask students to share some of their questions with the class.

★ **Mega Meetings** (page 56)—Ask each student to read the informational text on page 56 with a pencil in hand. Explain that they should circle any parts of the text they find confusing. After they finish reading, place the students in small groups. Tell students to work with their groups to clarify the text they circled. Have students stay in their groups and discuss the question: *Is it fair that the presidential candidate gets to choose the vice presidential nominee?* After students have discussed the question with their groups, have a class discussion. Encourage students to support their opinions on the matter.

★ **Convention Brackets** (page 57)—Students will use information from both the reader's theater script and the informational text to complete the bracket diagram on this page. After students have completed the brackets, have them share their sentences with peers.

★ **Building a Brochure** (page 58)—With this activity, students will use the checklist to design a brochure for a National Convention. If available, provide examples of brochures for students to view during this activity. When students have finished their brochures, display them around the classroom.

The National Convention *(cont.)*

Primary Source Connection

★ **Time to Celebrate Primary Source** (pages 59–60)—Study the primary source on page 59 with students. Read the background information as a class. Place all students' names in a hat and have each student pull the name of a classmate. Have them complete page 60 independently. Tell students to address their postcards to the classmate they pulled. Encourage them to be creative. When students have finished, have them deliver their postcards to their classmates.

Puzzle Time!

★ **What's that Word? Vocabulary Puzzle** (page 61)—Students will enjoy trying to unscramble National Convention vocabulary words.

★ **Convention Letter Tiles Puzzle** (page 62)—Students will have fun creating as many words as they can in 10 minutes using the letters in the tiles. Set a timer for 10 minutes. Write the words students come up with on the board. See which student has the most words.

Answer Key

Convention Brackets (page 57)

Student answers will vary but may include the following National Convention activities: selecting a chairperson; nominating a candidate; party platform is announced; keynote speaker; presidential candidate's speech; vice president is announced; balloon drop; people coming together; or people supporting their parties

What's that Word? Vocabulary Puzzle (page 61)

1. representatives
2. platform
3. nominate
4. keynote speaker
5. delegates
6. convention
7. chairperson
8. running mate

Convention Letter Tiles Puzzle (page 62)

Possible words include:

delegates	celebrate
national	fun
chairperson	loud
keynote speaker	speeches
running mate	president
platform	celebrities
official	United States
nominate	Democratic
songs	Republican
sing	primary
posters	elections
balloons	busy
party	hectic

★ ★ ★ Covering the Convention ★ ★ ★

Reporter: Good morning, Portland! I'm reporting from sunny Orlando, Florida. We are down here at the Republican National Convention. More than 50,000 people have flocked to this city. And they aren't here to see Mickey. They are here to . . .

Producer: Cut! Stop! Wait! There's a kid making faces behind you. Let's start again. Oh, and you may want to lose the Mickey joke. It's pretty cheesy.

Reporter: (*sighing*) Whatever you say, Boss! Tell me when to start.

Producer: And three, two, . . . (*pointing to the reporter*)

Reporter: Good Morning, Portland! Trudy Truman down here in sunny Orlando, Florida. I'm reporting from the bustling Republican National Convention. Over 50,000 people have come to the convention over the past three days. Here's one now. Excuse me, Miss? I'm Trudy Truman with the Portland, Maine, news team. May I ask you a few questions?

Woman: Of course.

Reporter: What have you learned the last few days here at the convention?

Woman: Well, I would have to say I learned what my party's platform really stands for. And I am proud to be a member of this party. I look forward to my party winning the election and improving our country.

Reporter: What has been your favorite part of the convention thus far?

Woman: I loved the keynote speaker. When I first learned that the speaker was a Hollywood actor, I was highly disappointed. But I have to say that his speech was the most informative and heartfelt of the whole convention.

Reporter: And finally, what are you looking forward to most in today's events?

Woman: I can't wait to hear our presidential candidate's speech. I'm eager to hear his plans for our country's future. I'm also dying to know who his vice presidential candidate will be!

Reporter: Thank you. The next time I speak to you fine people in Portland will be at the end of the convention tonight. We will be reporting live after the balloons have dropped and the crowds have calmed. Until then, this is Trudy Truman signing off.

Producer: Well done, Trudy.

★ ★ ★ **Covering the Convention** *(cont.)* ★ ★ ★

Directions: Imagine you are the news reporter covering the convention instead of Trudy Truman. Who would you interview? What questions would you ask?

I would want to interview _____ .

I would ask these three questions:

1. _____

_____

_____

2. _____

_____

_____

3. _____

_____

_____

Directions: Now, write an answer you would hope to get for one of the questions above.

_____

_____

_____

_____

★ ★ ★ Mega Meetings ★ ★ ★

National Conventions are huge political meetings. They happen in the same year a new president is chosen. Each political party has a convention. The two major conventions are the Republican National Convention and Democratic National Convention.

The conventions are in the summer. But they happen on different days. Each one lasts four days. They can be held in any city in the United States. Each party chooses its own location.

Each party has representatives that attend. They are called delegates. Party leaders and party supporters go, too. Sometimes, even celebrities and past presidents go!

First, a chairperson is selected. It is often the party's leader from the House of Representatives. It is this person's job to tell the crowd what will take place and when.

Delegates have a job, too. They have to nominate a candidate. This means they vote for who will run for president. But everyone already knows who will get chosen. This is because the citizens in each state choose. They vote in primary elections. The winner of the primary

election is the person who runs for president. The delegates just make it official. They represent their states' votes.

At the convention, a party platform will be announced. A platform is a party's ideas and beliefs. It states a party's goals for the country.

There are also lots and lots of speeches. There will be a keynote speaker, too. This person is often someone very famous. He or she will give a big speech. This gets the crowd excited.

The presidential candidate will give a big speech, too. The candidate will share the plans he or she has for the country. The candidate will also make a big announcement. The candidate will tell everyone who his or her running mate will be. If the candidate wins the election, this running mate will become the vice president!

During the convention, songs are sung. Music is played. Posters are shown. Signs are waved in the air. People cheer and dance. Balloons are dropped from the ceiling. It is like a big party.

The conventions give people a chance to support their candidates. They get people excited!

Directions: At the National Conventions, the presidential nominee gets to choose the vice presidential nominee. On Election Day, you have to vote for the two together. Do you think it is fair that the presidential nominee gets to make that choice? Why or why not?

Name _____ Date _____

See How They Run

★ ★ ★ **Convention Brackets** ★ ★ ★

Directions: Use what you learned from both texts to fill in the brackets below. List four important things that happen at the National Conventions. Next, narrow down that list to the two that you think are the most important. In the last box, list the one item that you feel is the most important of all. Then, write a few sentences explaining why you feel that is the most important event at each National Convention.

© Shell Education

#51353—Understanding Elections

57

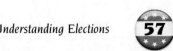

★ ★ ★ **Building a Brochure** ★ ★ ★

Directions: The National Conventions are big events. There is a lot that has to be done in the four days. Each party wants people to attend its convention and watch it on TV. Pick a party and create a brochure for its National Convention. Be sure your brochure is colorful, fun, and informative. Use the checklist below to help you!

Cover

❑ name of the political party

❑ dates of the convention

❑ location of the convention

❑ a catchy slogan

❑ fun graphics or pictures

Inside Cover

❑ paragraph stating party's platform

❑ biography and picture of keynote speaker

Inside Back Cover

❑ detailed schedule of events with times

Back Cover

❑ You choose! Be creative. A few ideas are listed below.

  ★ a map showing where the convention will be held

  ★ suggested hotels to stay in

  ★ suggested places to eat

  ★ suggested activities to do in town

★ ★ ★ **Time to Celebrate Primary Source** ★ ★ ★

Primary Source Background Information

These two pictures show the Republican National Convention in 1976. It took place in August. It was held in Kansas City, Missouri. The picture on the left shows delegates. They are waving posters. They show their support for Gerald Ford.

The picture on the right shows President Ford. He was officially nominated as the Republican candidate. He is with his wife, First Lady Betty Ford. He is also with his vice-presidential candidate Robert Dole and his wife Elizabeth. They are celebrating their nominations with balloons and speeches.

John T. Bledsoe, Library of Congress

★ ★ ★ # Time to Celebrate Primary Source (cont.) ★ ★ ★

Directions: Based on the two primary source pictures and background information, why are the National Conventions still important? Create a postcard. Draw a picture from a convention on the front. On the back, write to a friend explaining why National Conventions are still important.

(front)

(back)

★ ★ ★ What's that Word? Vocabulary Puzzle ★ ★ ★

Directions: Use the definitions to help you unscramble the vocabulary words.

1. e v r e s e p r t a t i e s n _____
    people who represent others

2. f l a t p m r o _____
    the official beliefs and goals of a political party or candidate

3. t e a m o n i n _____
    to officially choose a person to run for political office

4. t o n e y k e   r a k e s p e _____
    the famous person who gives an entertaining speech

5. l e d s t e g e a _____
    people appointed to vote for others

6. n o v c o e n i n t _____
    a large meeting of people

7. n o s p r e h a r i c _____
    a person who leads a meeting or event

8. n r u n n g i   t a m e _____
    the person who runs with someone else in an
    election but has a less important role

Name _____   Date _____

★ ★ ★ Convention Letter Tiles Puzzle ★ ★ ★

Directions: Use the letters on the letter tiles to make words that are related to the National Conventions. You can use each letter as many times as you would like. See how many words you can make in 10 minutes. Ready, set, go!

E   O   D   B   P   S   Y   M   T   R

A   I   U   C   H   N   G   K   F   L

_____   _____

_____   _____

_____   _____

_____   _____

_____   _____

_____   _____

_____   _____

_____   _____

_____   _____

_____   _____

The Campaign Trail

Standards

 Students will know how the values and principles of American democracy can be promoted through participating in government (e.g., voting, keeping informed about public issues, writing to legislators, serving on juries).

 Students will analyze fiction and nonfiction texts and synthesize the information in a variety of ways.

Paired Texts Reading and Activities

★ **My Campaign Journal** (pages 65–66)—Have students read My Campaign Journal in pairs. Next, go over the directions on page 66. Instruct students to complete this page with their partners. Afterwards, ask student volunteers to share their character traits and examples. Discuss with the class the characteristics of being a good citizen and why it is important to participate in the election process.

★ **Time to Hit the Road!** (page 67)—Read the informational text with students. Tell students to write a number next to each thing a candidate does on the campaign trail. Ask them to share some of the things they numbered. Talk about the importance of a good campaign slogan. Give examples of slogans from past elections. For example: Yes we can (Obama); I like Ike (Eisenhower); Who but Hoover? (Hoover); Happy Days Are Here Again! (FDR). Finally, have students imagine they are running for president and write their own campaign slogans. Ask volunteers to share their slogans with the class.

★ **Campaigning Counts** (page 68)—In this activity, students will use information from both the journal and informational text to answer text dependent questions. When students have finished, go over the answers as a class. Have students explain where in the text they found the answers.

★ **Creating a Job Ad** (page 69)—With this activity, students will imagine they are running for the presidency. They will need to assemble a strong team of volunteers to help them campaign. To do this, students will create job ads that can be placed online.

The Campaign Trail (cont.)

Primary Source Connection

★ **Super Hero Campaign Primary Source** (pages 70–71)—Study the primary source and read the background information with students. Read the directions on page 71 and have students complete their campaign posters. When students finish, place their campaign posters around the room. Ask student volunteers to share their slogans with the class.

Puzzle Time!

★ **Riddle in the Middle Vocabulary Puzzle** (page 72)—Students will enjoy figuring out the missing letters in the vocabulary words and using them to solve the riddle.

★ **Symbols and Slogans Puzzle** (page 73)—Students will have fun swapping the symbols for letters to decode campaign slogans.

Answer Key

My Campaign Journal (page 66)

Students' answers will vary but may include:

    Name: Jorge Garcia

    Trait 1: good citizen because he's interested in the upcoming election

    Trait 2: hard worker because he states how hard it is to work on the campaign but doesn't give up

    Trait 3: passionate because he was excited when he met Senator Jari

Campaigning Counts (page 68)

Students' answers will vary but may include:

1. a series of activities that candidates do during an election; they travel the country; they learn what people need; they give speeches
2. to get people to know them better; to win people's votes; so people know what they stand for and what they believe in
3. they make phone calls; they pass out stickers, buttons, and fliers; they write slogans; they make posters and signs

Bonus: Answers may vary but could include that it is a sign of a good citizen to be involved.

Creating a Job Ad (page 69)

Students' answers will vary but may include:

Introduction: I am a Senator running for president in the upcoming election. I want to help those in need and improve the educational system. To find out more about my platform, please see my website.

Job description: I am looking for someone to help with my campaign. This person will make buttons, posters, signs, brochures, etc., under my guidance and leadership.

Skills needed: good leadership skills; organized; hard worker; determined; politically minded

Riddle in the Middle Vocabulary Puzzle (page 72)

1. volunteer
2. fund-raiser
3. campaign
4. debates
5. opponent
6. strategy
7. lobbyists
8. slogan

Riddle Answer: Victoria Woodhull

Symbols and Slogans Puzzle (page 73)

Keep Cool with Coolidge

I Like Ike

Challenge: Calvin Coolidge and Dwight Eisenhower

★ ★ ★ My Campaign Journal ★ ★ ★

February 3

Last week in the primary elections, I voted for Senator Mateo Jari. I remember when he first announced that he would be running for president. I was thrilled! We share the same viewpoints on many issues.

March 27

Today I met with one of Senator Jari's field directors. After speaking with her, I decided to volunteer. I joined the campaign! I start tomorrow. I am very excited.

July 30

I have been working on Senator Jari's campaign for about four months now. I have learned so much about our political system. I never realized the amount of work that goes into a campaign. All the volunteers, myself included, have been busy. We call voters. We go door-to-door to gain support for the campaign. We inform voters of Senator Jari's views. We answer any questions they have.

August 15

I am tired—so tired! We are working nonstop! We are creating flyers and posters. We are making buttons and signs. We hand them out to the people we meet. We are also packing them in boxes to take them to the National Convention. I've never been to a National Convention. I bet it's going to be fun!

September 7

Just got home from the National Convention. It was great! There was so much excitement in the air. The crowd went crazy when Senator Jari accepted the nomination. Hundreds of balloons fell from the ceiling. But the best part was getting to meet Senator Jari. That was amazing! I, Jorge Garcia, met Senator Jari! I still can't believe it.

October 4

It is no secret that campaign volunteers work hard. But the candidates work hard, too. Senator Jari has been travelling nonstop since last year. He's met with many different people. He's participated in debates. He's given tons of speeches. He's done lots of interviews. He was even on *The Tonight Show*! I hope all this hard work pays off next month!

November 4, Part 1

It's ELECTION DAY!!! I went to my polling place first thing this morning. I proudly cast my vote for Jari.

November 4, Part 2

Although the day is not over yet, it looks like Senator Jari is going to win! They are predicting he will be the next president. I now know why it is so important to take part in our government. Volunteering on the campaign was a great experience. I learned so much and I feel like I made a difference.

November 5

It's official! President Jari's first day in office will be January 20! I can't wait for Inauguration Day!

★★★ My Campaign Journal *(cont.)* ★★★

Directions: What can you tell about the person writing this journal? What character traits does he have? Fill in the graphic organizer below to show what you know.

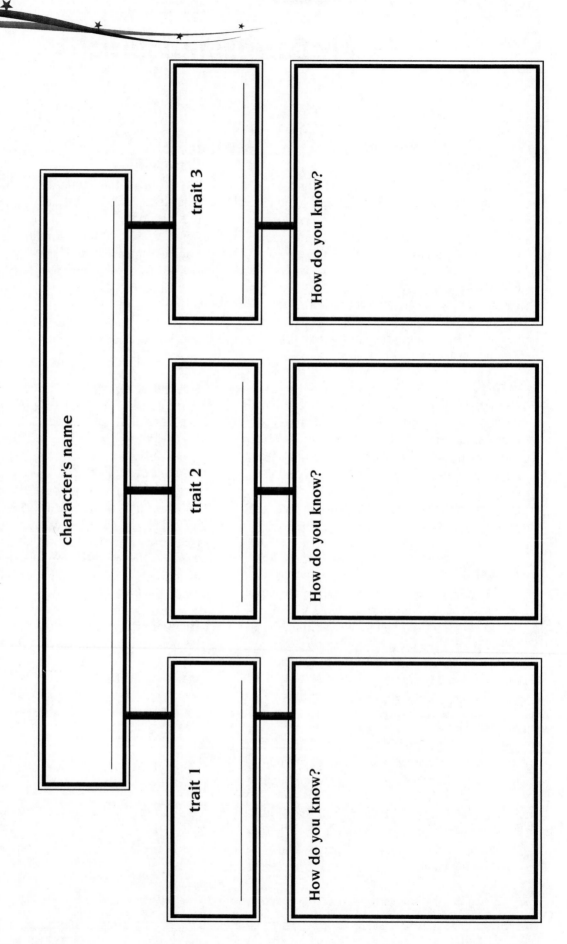

character's name

trait 1 — **How do you know?**

trait 2 — **How do you know?**

trait 3 — **How do you know?**

★ ★ ★ Time to Hit the Road! ★ ★ ★

How do you get people to vote for you to be the next president? You campaign! The goal of a campaign is to get a candidate's message out to the voters. The candidate needs to convince the voters that he or she is the best person for the job.

Campaigning involves a great deal of planning. You need good strategies. You must have a dedicated team to help you. Oh, and did I mention the traveling? There's lots of it! So pack your bags!

Most people who run for president belong to a party. There are two main political parties. One is the Republican Party. The other is the Democratic Party. On Election Day, only one candidate will represent each party. But many people from the same party may want to run for president. So there are primary elections. Candidates campaign to win the primaries. However, the real campaigning starts after the primary election.

The winners from the primaries now hit the road. The march on the campaign trail has begun. The candidates hold fund-raisers. This will raise money to help pay for the campaigns. Campaigns cost a lot of money.

People give money to campaigns. They do this because they hope the candidates will support their issues when elected.

During the campaign, the candidates travel around the country to visit as many different cities and states as they can. They talk to the voters and give speeches. They do interviews with reporters and appear on TV shows and radio stations. They create websites and may even send out Tweets!

Candidates take part in debates on TV, too. They argue their points with their opponents. They also make TV advertisements. Some advertisements tell and show what the candidate stands for and believes in. Other advertisements say what is wrong with the candidates' opponents.

There are also slogans, signs, and buttons! A candidate's campaign team works hard to make all these items. The team consists of a lot of volunteers. These are people who help for free because they believe in the candidates.

If a campaign is successful, then that candidate may be elected the next president!

Directions: Campaign slogans are important. They help voters remember the candidates. Imagine that you are running for president. Write your own campaign slogan. Remember these tips: keep it short, simple, and catchy. Make sure it is memorable!

★ ★ ★ **Campaigning Counts** ★ ★ ★

Directions: Use both texts to help you answer the questions below. Give specific examples from both texts to support your answers.

1. What is a campaign?

_____

_____

_____

2. Why do candidates campaign?

_____

_____

_____

3. How do volunteers help candidates campaign?

_____

_____

_____

Bonus!

Why is it important for citizens to get involved in the campaign process?

_____

_____

_____

Name _____ Date _____

★ ★ ★ Creating a Job Ad ★ ★ ★

Directions: Imagine you are running for president. Think about the kind of character traits and skills you want your volunteers to have. Create a job posting below that will go on the Internet. Tell about yourself and why you are running for president. Then, describe the job the volunteer will be doing. Next, include the character traits and skills the volunteer will need to have to get the job done.

Volunteers Needed

Introduction

_____

_____

_____

Job Description

_____

_____

_____

Skills Needed

_____

_____

_____

_____

_____

★ ★ ★ Super Hero Campaign Primary Source ★ ★ ★

Primary Source Background Information

Campaigns are full of buttons, signs, posters, banners, and slogans! Days before the election, there are commercials for candidates all over the TV. There may be signs and posters all over your neighborhood. Slogans will be stuck in your head. You will see people wearing buttons. Campaign hype will be everywhere!

This is a DC Comics™ book cover from 1943. It shows Wonder Woman running for president. There are many aspects of a typical campaign in the picture. Wonder Woman is giving a speech to a crowd. There are signs supporting her. People are cheering. However, there is also a sign in the crowd. It says, "Wonder Woman 1000 Years in the Future!" This suggests that some people felt the United States was not ready for a woman president in 1943.

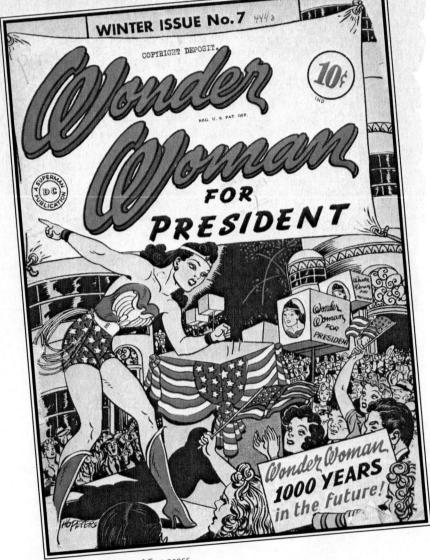

H.G. Peter, Library of Congress

Name _____ Date _____

★ ★ ★ **Super Hero Campaign Primary Source** *(cont.)* ★ ★ ★

Directions: Pick your favorite super hero or create your own! Design a campaign poster for the super hero. Then, write a slogan for your super hero's campaign! Be clever and creative.

_____

_____

_____

★ ★ ★ Riddle in the Middle Vocabulary Puzzle ★ ★ ★

Directions: Use the definitions and the Word Bank to help you fill in the missing letters in the vocabulary words. Then, write the letter in the middle of each set of parentheses on a line at the bottom of the page to solve the riddle.

1. doing something for free without being forced

(__) ___ ___ ___ n ___ e   e ___

2. an event held to collect money for a political party

f ___ ___ d - r ___ (__) ___ ___ r

3. steps taken by candidates to get them elected

(__) ___ m ___ ___ i   g ___

4. discussions in which ideas are given for or against issues

___ ___ b ___ (__) ___ s

5. a person who is running against another person in a campaign

(__) p   p ___ ___ ___ ___ t

6. a plan to achieve a goal

___ t (__) ___ t ___ ___ y

7. people who try to persuade politicians to vote for bills they favor

___ ___ b   b ___ (__) ___ ___ s

8. a word or phrase that is easy to remember and is used to attract attention to a campaign

___ l ___ ___ (__) n

Word Bank
campaign
debates
fund-raiser
lobbyists
opponent
slogan
strategy
volunteer

Who was the first woman to run for president?

___ ___ ___ ___ ___ ___ ___ ___ Woodhull

★ ★ ★ Symbols and Slogans Puzzle ★ ★ ★

Directions: Use the key to swap symbols for letters and figure out two of the most famous campaign slogans in history.

C = Φ	H = ♪	O = ⌫
D = #	I = ∞	P = ⌘
E = π	K = ✚	T = ✪
G = ¥	L = ★	W = ❖

Slogan 1

✚ π π ⌘   Φ ⌫ ⌫ ★   ❖ ∞ ✪ ♪

___ ___ ___ ___   ___ ___ ___ ___   ___ ___ ___ ___

Φ ⌫ ⌫ ★ ∞ # ¥ π

___ ___ ___ ___ ___ ___ ___ ___

Slogan 2

∞   ★ ∞ ✚ π   ∞ ✚ π

___   ___ ___ ___ ___   ___ ___ ___

Challenge!

To which presidential candidates do these slogans belong?

_____

Presidential Debates

Standards

☑ Students know how the values and principles of American democracy can be promoted through participating in government (e.g., voting, keeping informed about public issues, writing to legislators, serving on juries).

☑ Students will analyze fiction and nonfiction texts and synthesize the information in a variety of ways.

Paired Texts Reading and Activities

★ **I'm Ready for My Close-up** (page 76)—Have students read a fictional account of the Kennedy/Nixon debate. Explain to students that this is a historical fiction story based on true events. Tell them that in the story, facts are mixed with fiction. Direct students to sketch Kennedy and Nixon based on the author's descriptions. Ask them to share their drawings with partners and discuss if they think it is fair that Vice President Nixon's debate skills were judged based on his appearance. After a few minutes, open the discussion to the class.

★ **Talk It Out** (pages 77–78)—Read the informational text with students. During the reading, tell students to circle the characteristics of a good debater. Next, discuss the importance of presidential debates as a class. Explain to students that it is up to the voters to stay informed on public issues and research the candidates' viewpoints. Instruct students to complete page 78 independently.

★ **3, 2, 1 Debate!** (page 79)— In this activity, students will use information from both the informational text and the historical fiction text to list facts and examples. They will also each write one opinion on debates. Students can complete the page individually or in pairs. When students have finished, have volunteers share their responses with the class.

★ **Debating the Issues** (page 80)— Place students in groups of three. Supply each group with a coin to flip and a timer. Go over the directions and steps on page 80 as a class. Then, have the groups complete the activity. After the groups have concluded their debates, ask student volunteers to share their experiences with the class. Discuss what topics they debated, which topics had the most heated debates, which topics were the easiest to debate, and what strategies debaters use.

Presidential Debates *(cont.)*

Primary Source Connection

★ **Lincoln-Douglas Debates Primary Source** (pages 81–82)—Study the primary source and read the background information with students. Go over the directions on page 82 as a class and have students complete the page independently. Ask for volunteers to share their three questions. Have volunteers explain why the answers to these questions are important to them.

Puzzle Time!

★ **All Mixed Up Vocabulary Puzzle** (page 83)—Students will enjoy placing the jumbled vocabulary words in the correct sentences.

★ **Debate Disaster Puzzle** (page 84)—Students will have fun trying to find hidden objects in this hilarious picture of a debate gone wild!

Answer Key

3, 2, 1 Debate! (page 79)

Student answers may vary but could include:

3 facts: there is a moderator; how a candidate acts is important; a candidate must know current events

2 examples: The moderator began the debate; some thought Nixon was nervous or lying because he was sweating so much, while others thought Nixon looked unkempt and sickly.

1 opinion: I think debates are important and informative because they are a good way to learn more about a candidates' beliefs and skills.

All Mixed Up Vocabulary Puzzle (page 83)

1. To win a debate, you should know the people you are debating against, your *opponents*, well.
2. In the Lincoln-Douglas debates, the two men shared their *viewpoints* on the topic of slavery.
3. In debates, *moderators* act as the referees and tell each person when to speak.
4. *Issues* discussed in a presidential debate can include the economy, the environment, and health care.

Debate Disaster Puzzle (page 84)

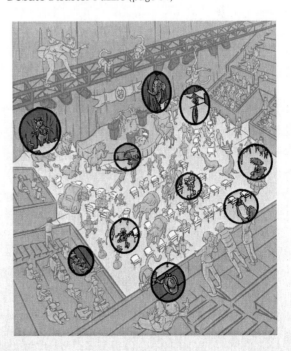

★ ★ ★ **I'm Ready for My Close-up** ★ ★ ★

"Wake up! It's time to go!" Ted shouted to John F. Kennedy.

"Can't I sleep for five more minutes?" said Kennedy while yawning, covered in notecards.

"Sure! If you want to miss the first presidential debate to be broadcast on television," mocked Ted.

Ted Sorenson was Kennedy's aide. He also helped write his speeches.

Kennedy's opponent was Vice President Richard Nixon. Nixon had just been released from the hospital. A few weeks beforehand he had cut his knee on a car door. The cut had gotten infected. He was sick but determined to go ahead with the debate.

"Vice President, may I apply powder to your face so you won't appear shiny on TV?" asked the timid makeup artist.

"Absolutely not. I do not wear makeup!" barked Nixon.

"Mr. Kennedy is wearing powder, Sir."

"I don't care what Mr. Kennedy does."

Nixon was tired and ill. Kennedy, however, looked young and dashing in his suit and was well rested.

The moderator began the debate. Bob Flemming from ABC News asked the first question. It was for Kennedy. It was about comments Nixon had made about him during the campaign.

"In his campaign he has said that you are naive and at times immature and has raised the question of leadership. On this issue, why do you think people should vote for you and not the vice president?" asked Bob.

Kennedy's answer was strong and well supported. He ended his statement with, "I think Mr. Nixon is an effective leader of his party. I hope he would grant me the same. The question before us is which point of view and which party do we want to lead the United States."

The lights in the TV studio were bright and hot. Nixon was sweating a lot. But he was able to answer questions he was asked and hold his own in the debate. Still, many people could not get past his looks. Some thought he was nervous or lying because he was sweating so much. Others thought he looked unkempt and sickly. On the other hand, Kennedy looked comfortable, relaxed, and healthy.

"I think you won that debate," Ted joyfully told Kennedy.

"Now, let's just hope I win the presidency!" replied Kennedy.

Directions: Use the author's descriptions to draw pictures of Kennedy and Nixon during the debate. Do you think it was fair that people judged Nixon's debating skills based on the way he looked? Share your opinion and drawings with a partner.

★ ★ ★ Talk It Out ★ ★ ★

Stop! Before you cast your vote, you must do your research and know your candidate well. Does your candidate support your viewpoints? Does your candidate hold some of the same values and beliefs that you do? Good citizens learn about their candidates. They read articles about their candidates online or in newspapers. They watch advertisements on the candidates. They listen to interviews with the candidates. A great way to learn a lot about candidates is by watching a debate on live television.

A debate is a discussion. It gives candidates a chance to express their ideas on issues. Each debate has a moderator. He or she is like a referee. The moderator asks a candidate a question about an issue. Then, the candidate has a few minutes to respond. When the candidate's time is up, it's the other candidate's turn. The two candidates go back and forth discussing why they are for or against each issue.

A candidate must know about current events. They need to know about the problems the world is facing. They also need to know about the problems America is facing. They should have a good understanding of United States history. This will allow them to use examples from the past. It will help them support their ideas.

In a debate, how a candidate acts is very important. Good debaters not only know what to say but how to say it. They remain calm and do not get upset. They do not yell, but they still show passion. This means they are excited to express their opinions, but they do it in a professional manner. They are critical, and they disagree with their opponents. However, they do it respectfully.

In 1960, the presidential debates were shown on TV for the first time. John F. Kennedy and Richard Nixon held four debates. Millions of voters watched the debates or listened to them on the radio. In the first debate, people noticed that Kennedy remained calm. He looked young and healthy. But Nixon was sweating a lot. He looked tired and gaunt. People thought he was nervous or ill. Those people felt that Kennedy won the debate. But the people that listened on the radio thought Nixon had won. The candidates' appearance made a difference in the opinions of voters.

You must watch debates closely. You must listen carefully. You must think hard about the issues being discussed. This will help you vote for the best person to lead our country.

★ ★ ★ Talk It Out (cont.)

Directions: Use the nonfiction text *Talk It Out* to complete the graphic organizer below.

What I thought while reading . . .

_____

I would like to learn more about . . .

Three big ideas include . . .

_____

My favorite part was . . .

_____

★ ★ ★ *3, 2, 1 Debate!* ★ ★ ★

Directions: Write **three** facts you learned from *Talk It Out*. Next, find where **two** of those facts were mentioned in *I'm Ready for My Close-up*. Then, write **one** opinion you have about debates in general.

3 facts from *Talk It Out*

1.	2.	3.

2 examples from *I'm Ready for My Close-up*

1.	2.

1 opinion on debates

1.

Name _____ Date _____

★ ★ ★ Debating the Issues ★ ★ ★

Directions: Work with your group to write the issues that are important to you in the left column. Next, write solutions for these issues in the right column. You should have at least three possible solutions for each issue. After you complete the table, follow the steps at the bottom of the page.

Issues	Solving the Issues
1.	★ ★ ★
2.	★ ★ ★
3.	★ ★ ★

Step 1: Assign one person in your group to be a moderator. The moderator will pick one topic from the list above. This is the topic the other two students will debate.

Step 2: Have the moderator flip a coin. The winner of the coin toss can decide if he or she will be *for* or *against* the issue that will be debated.

Step 3: The winner of the coin toss will go first. This student will have one minute to discuss the issue. After the minute is up, it is the second student's turn to respond. This student has 30 seconds. The moderator will be in charge of the timer.

Step 4: Now, switch roles. The new moderator will pick a new topic and follow Steps 2–3. Do this one more time so that everyone in your group has had a turn to be a moderator and all topics have been debated.

★ ★ ★ Lincoln-Douglas Debates Primary Source ★ ★ ★

Primary Source Background Information

In 1858, great debates took place in Illinois. They are some of the most famous debates in history. Senator Stephen A. Douglas and Abraham Lincoln held seven debates. The debates were held in seven different cities in Illinois. They were running for the office of senator from Illinois. Senator Douglas was short and stocky. He wore fancy clothes. He spoke eloquently. Lincoln was tall and lanky. He wore plain clothes. He spoke frankly.

The main issue in the debates was slavery. Lincoln's arguments were clear and direct. This made him famous.

Lincoln lost the election for senator. But he got more votes in the counties where the debates were held than he did in the other counties. And he emerged as a leader of the new Republican Party.

This poster shows just how popular the debates were. This poster is from the late 1930s. DuPage County in Illinois was celebrating its 100th anniversary. They did so by reenacting the Lincoln-Douglas debates.

Ill[inois] : Federal Art Proj., WPA, Library of Congress

★ ★ ★ Lincoln-Douglas Debates Primary Source (cont.) ★ ★ ★

Directions: Presidential debates are great ways for voters to get to know their candidates. They can make or break a candidate's campaign. Write three questions you would like to ask a presidential candidate today during a debate. Explain why the answers to the questions are important to you.

My Questions

1. _____

_____

_____

2. _____

_____

_____

3. _____

_____

_____

These answers are important to me because

_____

_____

_____

_____

★ ★ ★ All Mixed Up Vocabulary Puzzle ★ ★ ★

Directions: Read the sentences below carefully. You will notice that the bold words are in the wrong sentences. They are all mixed up! Rewrite the sentences using the correct bolded word for each one.

1. To win a debate, you should know the people you are debating against, your **moderators**, well.

2. In the Lincoln-Douglas debates, the two men shared their **issues** on the topic of slavery.

3. In debates, **opponents** act as the referees and tell each person when to speak.

4. **Viewpoints** discussed in a presidential debate can include the economy, the environment, and health care.

1. _____

_____

_____

2. _____

_____

_____

3. _____

_____

_____

4. _____

_____

_____

Name _____ Date _____

★ ★ ★ Debate Disaster Puzzle ★ ★ ★

Directions: This debate has gone wild! Animals from the circus next door broke free and interrupted the debate! Find these hidden objects in the chaotic picture below.

| guitar | cowboy hat | star balloon | donkey | pizza slice |
| umbrella | unicycle | cell phone | elephant | megaphone |

© *Shell Education*

Election Day

 Standards

☑ Students know the fundamental principles of American democracy (e.g., the people are sovereign; the power of government is limited by law; people exercise their authority directly through voting; people exercise their authority indirectly through elected representatives).

☑ Students will analyze fiction and nonfiction texts and synthesize the information in a variety of ways.

Paired Texts Reading and Activities

★ **A Funny Thing Happened on the Way to the Polls** (pages 87–88)—Instruct students to read the comic on page 87. Discuss the problem and the solution in the story as a class. Next, have students complete page 88 independently. Ask for volunteers to share their new endings with the class. Have students explain why they chose the endings they did.

★ **The People's Choice** (page 89)—Read the informational text as a class. During the reading, instruct students to circle the parts they found to be the most interesting. Ask a few students to share their favorite parts with the class and explain why they chose those parts. Then place students in small groups and have them write songs or raps that will inspire voters to head to the polls.

★ **Breaking It Down** (page 90)—In this activity, students will use information from both the informational text and the comic to complete the graphic organizer. Students can complete the page individually or in pairs. When students have finished, have volunteers share their responses with the class.

★ **Candidate Characteristics** (page 91)—With this activity, students will write paragraphs explaining the characteristics they think the candidate in the comic possesses that won the man's vote. Encourage students to include characteristics that they would like their ideal candidates to have, as well.

Election Day (cont.)

Primary Source Connection

★ **Get Out and Vote! Primary Source** (pages 92–93)—Study the primary source and read the background information on page 92 with students. Then, have students complete page 93 independently. Explain to students that they will choose a freedom that is important to them. Tell them that they will then write or draw why that freedom is important and how voting protects that freedom. When students have finished, go over students' answers as a class.

Puzzle Time!

★ **Election Day Diamond Vocabulary Puzzle** (page 94)—Students will enjoy finding the hidden vocabulary words in the diamond-shaped puzzle.

★ **Blustery Ballot Puzzle** (page 95)—Students will have fun getting through the maze to get the voter's ballot back after it blew away in the wind.

Answer Key

Breaking It Down (page 90)

A Funny Thing Happened on the Way to the Polls	Both	The People's Choice
Problem The man is trying to get to the polling place to vote, but his car broke down.	**Main Idea** Voting in Elections	**Fact About Polling Places** they can be at schools, libraries, or other public buildings
Solution The candidate the man is voting for picks him up and gives him a ride to the polling place.	**New Words I Learned** civic duty ballots voting booths	**Fact About Ballots** Some ballots are on paper and others are on machines.

Election Day Diamond Puzzle Vocabulary Puzzle (page 94)

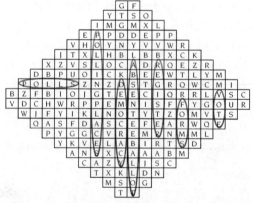

Blustery Ballot Puzzle (page 95)

★★★ A Funny Thing Happened on the Way to the Polls ★★★

★★★ A Funny Thing Happened on the Way to the Polls (cont.) ★★★

Directions: Imagine the main character did not get a lift from candidate Arroz. How could he get to the polling place to vote? Create a new ending below. You can cut out the speech bubbles below and use them in your comic.

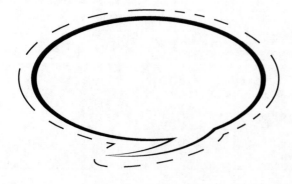

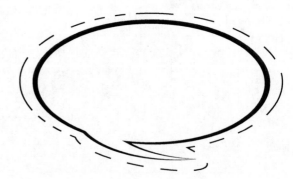

★ ★ ★ The People's Choice ★ ★ ★

The United States is a democracy. This means we the people choose our leaders. We do this by voting in elections. The power belongs to the people. Voting is a right for citizens.

Presidential elections are held every four years. Election Day is always on the Tuesday following the first Monday in November. This was decided when many people had to make long journeys to the polling places. By early November, the crops were in. The weather was not too hot or too cold. So voters could begin their journeys on Monday. They would get to the booths by Tuesday to vote.

In order to vote, you must be 18. You must also be registered to vote. You can register online. Or you can mail in the forms to register. You can pick up the forms at public libraries and post offices. Government offices have the forms, too. Some states even allow voters to register on Election Day at the polls.

Voters cast their ballots at polling places. Polling places can be at schools, libraries, and other public buildings. Each voter is assigned a polling place. People can also vote using absentee ballots. This type of ballot lets people send in their votes by mail. Some states require a reason for an absentee ballot. Reasons may include travel or sickness. Citizens living outside the United States can use absentee ballots, too. But a voter must request an absentee ballot before the election occurs.

Some polling places use paper ballots. Voters fill out ballots using pens. Other polling places use computers or machines. On all ballots, each presidential candidate runs together with the vice-presidential candidate. But how do citizens know who to vote for?

Citizens should vote for the candidates who share the same values they do. This means they believe in many of the same things. Voters should also look for certain personal traits. Strong candidates believe in the ideas of the Constitution. They respect the rights of others. They are reliable. They should be smart, honest, and hard working. They should also have experience working in government.

It is important for citizens to vote. It is their civic duty. It is a way for their voices to be heard. Sometimes, elections can be very close. Every vote can make a difference.

Directions: It is up to you to convince people to vote in the next election. Write a song or a rap that will inspire voters to head to the polls. If you would like, you can set your song to a familiar tune such as "Yankee Doodle" or "Twinkle, Twinkle, Little Star."

Name _____ Date _____

★ ★ ★ Breaking It Down ★ ★ ★

Directions: Use A *Funny Thing Happened on the Way to the Polls* and *The People's Choice* to fill in the graphic organizer below.

A Funny Thing Happened on the Way to the Polls	Both	The People's Choice
Problem	Main Idea	Fact about Polling Places
_____	_____	_____
_____	_____	_____
_____	_____	_____
_____	_____	_____
_____	_____	_____
_____	_____	_____
_____	_____	_____
Solution	New Words I Learned	Fact about Ballots
_____	_____	_____
_____	_____	_____
_____	_____	_____
_____	_____	_____
_____	_____	_____
_____	_____	_____

★ ★ ★ **Candidate Characteristics** ★ ★ ★

Directions: In A *Funny Thing Happened on the Way to the Polls*, the main character does not mention why he is voting for candidate Arroz. Using what you learn from *The People's Choice*, write a paragraph about the traits you think candidate Arroz has that help her win the election. Include traits that you would want your next president to have.

_____

_____

_____

_____

_____

_____

_____

_____

_____

_____

_____

_____

_____

_____

_____

★ ★ ★ Get Out and Vote! Primary Source ★ ★ ★

Primary Source Background Information

This poster was created in 1943. This was during World War II. It reminds Americans of the importance of voting. It encourages them to exercise their right to vote. The poster shows a hand reaching to press the lever on a voting machine. The levers on the machine read "Freedom of Enterprise," "Freedom of Worship," "Freedom of Speech," and "Freedom of Press." The poster shows that voting can protect those freedoms.

Library of Congress

★ ★ ★ **Get Out and Vote! Primary Source** *(cont.)* ★ ★ ★

Directions: Voting protects our freedoms. Choose one of the freedoms from the primary source image, listed in the box. Or choose another freedom you have. Write or draw why that freedom is important to you. Include how voting protects that freedom for you. Use books and the Internet to help you research your answers.

┌───┐
│   **Freedoms**   │
│   │
│   Freedom of Enterprise   Freedom of Worship│
│   │
│   Freedom of Speech   Freedom of Press │
└───┘

Name _____   Date _____

★★★ Election Day Diamond Vocabulary Puzzle ★★★

Directions: Find the words listed at the bottom of the page in the diamond.

```
                        G   F
                    Y   T   S   O
                I   M   G   M   X   L
            E   P   P   D   D   E   P   P
        V   H   O   Y   N   Y   V   V   W   R
    J   T   X   L   H   B   L   B   B   X   C   K
  X   Z   V   S   L   O   C   A   D   R   Q   E   Z   R
D   B   P   U   O   I   C   K   B   E   E   W   T   L   Y   M
P   O   L   L   S   Z   N   Z   D   S   T   G   R   Q   W   C   M   I
B   Z   F   B   I   O   J   G   T   E   E   C   I   Q   R   R   L   V   S   C
V   D   C   H   W   R   P   P   E   M   N   I   S   F   F   Y   G   O   U   R
  W   J   F   Y   I   K   L   N   O   T   Y   T   Z   O   M   V   T   S
      Q   A   S   F   D   A   S   C   E   F   E   A   R   W   Q   E
          P   Y   G   G   C   V   R   E   M   R   N   M   M   L
              Y   K   V   E   L   A   B   I   R   T   S   D
                  A   N   S   X   C   A   A   A   B   M
                      C   A   Z   Y   L   J   S   C
                          T   X   K   L   D   N
                              M   S   O   G
                                  T   T
```

democracy	absentee ballot	forms
polling places	polls	register	vote

★ ★ ★ **Blustery Ballot Puzzle** ★ ★ ★

Directions: Be a good citizen and help the woman catch her ballot that blew away in the wind.

The Electoral College

Standards

☑ Students know ways people can influence the decisions and actions of their government such as voting; taking an active role in interest groups, political parties, and other organizations that attempt to influence public policy and elections; attending meetings of governing agencies (e.g., city council); working in campaigns, circulating and signing petitions; and contributing money to political parties, candidates, or causes.

☑ Students will analyze fiction and nonfiction texts and synthesize the information in a variety of ways.

Paired Texts Reading and Activities

★ **Still Counting** (page 98)—Direct students to read the fictional newspaper article, Still Counting. Review the Electoral College and its role in elections. Discuss as a class how close the fictional election is and how it's important that people vote in order to have an influence on the government. Have student pairs discuss whether it is fair that a president can win the popular vote but lose the election. Ask students to share their discussions.

★ **Finding Out Who Won** (pages 99–100)—Have students read the informational text and circle words in the text they find tricky or confusing. Go over and clarify these words as a class. Tell students to complete the first column on page 100. Then, place students in small groups and have them complete the rest of the graphic organizer. Ask students to share words that they could not define in their groups. Work together as a class to define each word and use it in a sentence.

★ **Finding Facts** (page 101)—In this activity, students will use information from both the informational text and the fictional newspaper article to complete the graphic organizer. Students can complete the page individually or in pairs. When students have finished, have volunteers share their responses with the class.

★ **Your Turn to Count** (page 102)—With this activity, students will use an Electoral College map to determine the winner of an election and answer the questions on page 102.

America Votes

The Electoral College *(cont.)*

Primary Source Connection

★ **D.C. Dilemma Primary Source** (pages 103–104)—Study the primary source and read the background information on page 103 with students. Then, go over page 104 with students and have them complete the page independently. Explain to them that they will create license plate slogans for Washington, D.C., to help with its fight to get more electoral votes.

Puzzle Time!

★ **Electoral College Crossword Puzzle** (page 105)—Students will enjoy completing the crossword puzzle that consists of Electoral College-related vocabulary words.

★ **Electoral Map Puzzle** (page 106)—Students will have fun solving math problems by using an Electoral College map.

Answer Key

Finding Facts (page 101)

Fact 1: A candidate must have at least 270 electoral votes to win.

Fact 2: A president winning the election but losing the popular vote has only happened four times in history.

Fact 3: The number of electoral votes a state has is based on its population.

Fact 4: To get rid of the Electoral College, a change would have to be made to the Constitution.

Your Turn to Count (page 102)

And the winner is Burns.

1. California because it has the most electoral votes.

2. Answers will vary based on where the student lives.
3. 3 electoral votes

Electoral College Crossword Puzzle (page 105)

Down
1. official
2. pledge
3. Senators
4. representatives
5. Amendment

Across
6. Electoral College (no space)
7. electoral votes (no space)
8. popular votes (no space)

Electoral Map Puzzle (page 106)
1. 70
2. 20
3. 31
4. 11
5. 9
6. 2
7. 0
8. 15
9. 11
10. 2

© Shell Education   #51353—Understanding Elections   **97**

★ ★ ★ Still Counting ★ ★ ★

By Currer Bell

Freedom Press
Staff Writer

Atlanta, Georgia — By now, we usually know who the next president will be. But this year, we do not. We are still waiting to see who won. The election is too close to call.

Thursday, it looked like candidate Barnes was going to win. He had the most votes. He was leading the popular vote with 48,591,577 votes. And he had the most electoral votes with 255. A candidate must have at least 270 electoral votes to win. He needed only 15 more electoral votes.

But then, the unthinkable happened! Barnes lost in Ohio. He lost in his home state. No one saw it coming. All 18 electoral votes for that state went to candidate Bello.

Bello is now leading the electoral vote with 267 votes. He only needs 3 more electoral votes to win. But he is still losing in the popular vote. He only has 46,789,987 votes.

Only one state is still counting its votes. And it is our state! Whoever wins Georgia will win the election. Our state has 16 electoral votes.

If Bello wins the election, he will make history. He will win the election on electoral votes. But he will not have the most popular votes. This has only happened four other times in history! The idea that this could happen is making many people mad. They think the candidate who wins the popular vote should win the election. But that is not what our Constitution says.

Our Constitution says that each state has a certain number of electoral votes. This number is based on how many people live in the state. The candidate that gets more than 270 electoral votes wins the election. To change this law, we would need to change the Constitution.

In the meantime, we sit and wait. Who will win Georgia's electoral votes? Who will be the next president? Barnes? Bello? The suspense is maddening!

Directions: Do you think it is fair that a president can win the popular vote but lose the election? Discuss this topic with a partner. Write your opinion and list three reasons that support your opinion.

★ ★ ★ Finding Out Who Won ★ ★ ★

Presidential elections can be tricky. Counting the votes is not easy. This is because there are two kinds of votes. There is the *popular vote*. This means the number of votes cast by citizens. There is also the *electoral vote*. This means the number of votes given to a candidate by each state. When people vote for a president, they are really voting for electors. This group of electors is called the Electoral College.

The number of electors in each state differs. Some states have lots of electors. Others have just a few. To find the number of electors for each state, you have to do some simple math. You add the number of senators to the number of representatives. Each state has two senators. But each state has a different number of representatives. The number of representatives is based on how many people live in the state. For example, Missouri has two senators. But it has eight representatives. You add eight plus two. So the state has 10 electors.

Electors take a pledge. They promise to be honest. They vote for the candidate who wins the popular vote in their state. Each elector casts one vote. States with more people have more electoral votes. Texas has 38 electoral votes. California has 55 electoral votes. Candidates really want to win these states. All those electoral votes can help them win the election.

Citizens cast their votes in November. A winner is usually announced in a couple days. But it is not made official until later. Electors cast their votes in December. The votes are then sent to Congress. On January 6, the votes are counted. The candidate that gets the most electoral votes wins. Now, it is official. It takes at least 270 electoral votes to win. If there is no winner in the Electoral College, then the House of Representatives chooses the president.

Sometimes a candidate can win the popular vote but lose the election. This means they did not get the most electoral votes. This has happened four times. The last candidate this happened to was Al Gore, who lost the 2000 election to George W. Bush. Because this can happen, many people do not like the Electoral College. They think the president should be chosen based on the popular vote alone. But it would not be easy to change this law. An amendment would have to be passed. This is a change to the Constitution. People have tried to do this more than 700 times! But it has yet to happen.

★ ★ ★ Finding Out Who Won (cont.) ★ ★ ★

Directions: Pick four words that you found tricky or confusing in the nonfiction text and use them to complete the graphic organizer below.

Word	Define It	Use It in a Sentence

★ ★ ★ Finding Facts ★ ★ ★

Directions: Use both texts to complete the graphic organizer below. The *Still Counting* text is fiction, but it does contain facts. Use the *Finding Out Who Won* text to help you find at least four facts in the fiction text.

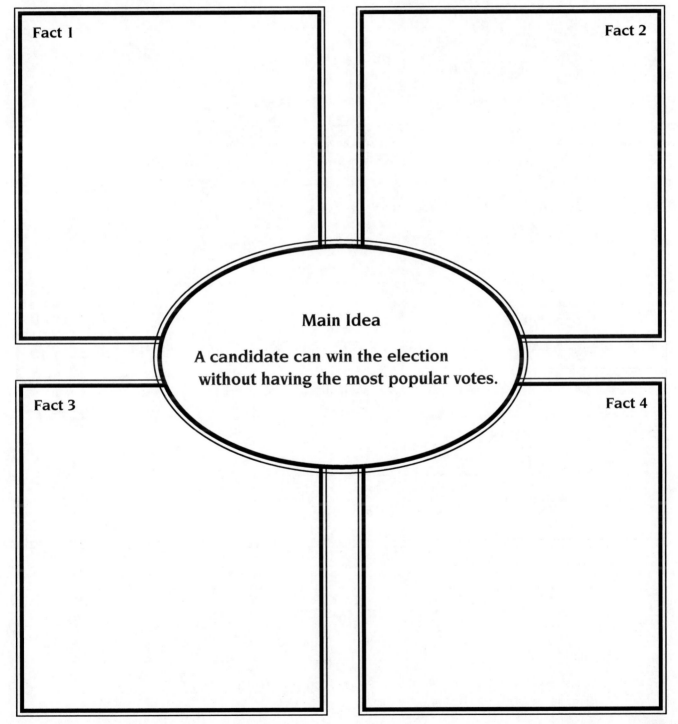

Fact 1

Fact 2

Main Idea

**A candidate can win the election
without having the most popular votes.**

Fact 3

Fact 4

Name _____ Date _____

★ ★ ★ Your Turn to Count ★ ★ ★

Directions: Study the map below. Use it to find out which candidate won the presidential election and to answer the questions below. Show your math on the back of this sheet.

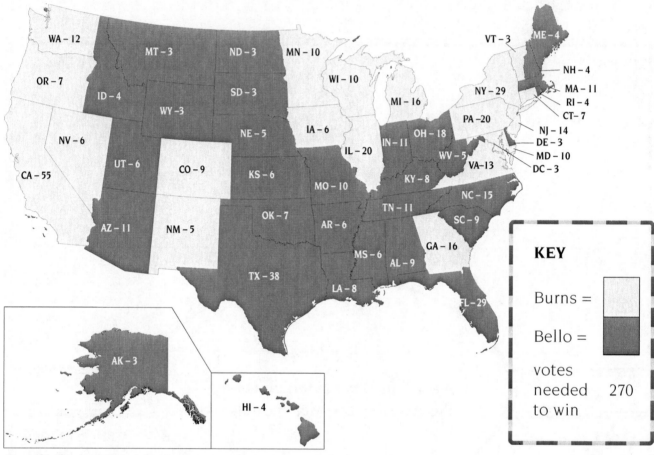

And the winner is . . .

_____

1. Which state has the highest population? How do you know?

_____

_____

2. How many electoral votes does your state have?

_____

3. What is the least amount of electoral votes a state has?

_____

★ ★ ★ D.C. Dilemma Primary Source ★ ★ ★

Primary Source Background Information

Did you know Washington, D.C., is not a state? It is a district. It is the District of Columbia. It is our nation's capital. But there is not a star on the flag for it. Over 600,000 people live in D.C. But they do not have representatives in Congress. They have no senators and only one non-voting representative. The residents of the District think this is unfair. But the Constitution says only states have these rights, and the District of Columbia is not a state.

In 1961, a change was made to the Constitution. The 23rd Amendment was added. It said the people living in D.C. could vote for president. Before the amendment, they were not allowed to vote, but now they have three electoral votes.

Today, many District residents are still upset. They want more electoral votes. And they want representatives and senators. If you visit the capital, look at the license plates on the cars. On them it says, "TAXATION WITHOUT REPRESENTATION." This is a reference to a famous slogan from before the American Revolution. It is what the colonists said to Great Britain. They had no representation in the British government, but they still had to pay taxes. So do the people living in Washington, D.C., today.

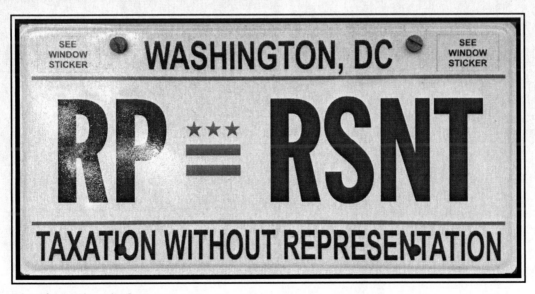

Edited from Wikimedia Commons

★ ★ ★ D.C. Dilemma Primary Source *(cont.)* ★ ★ ★

Directions: Many people who live in D.C. want representation in Congress, and they want more electoral votes. They came up with a clever license plate slogan to help bring attention to their cause. Design another clever license plate slogan that residents of D.C. could use, and create your license plate.

WASHINGTON, DC

ABC 1234

★★★ Electoral College Crossword Puzzle ★★★

Directions: Use the clues to complete the puzzle with the words in the Word Bank.

Word Bank

Ammendment
Electoral College
electoral votes
official
pledge
popular votes
representatives
Senators

Down

1. something that is done in a public and formal way

2. a serious promise or agreement

3. members of the Senate

4. people who represent others in Congress

Across

5. the body of electors who formally elect the president and vice president

6. a law or statement added to the Constitution

7. votes cast in the Electoral College by electors

8. votes cast by the public or citizens of a nation

Name _____ Date _____

★ ★ ★ Electoral Map Puzzle ★ ★ ★

Directions: Use the map and find the number of each state's electoral votes to solve the math equations. Be sure to make sure that your answers are part of the Answer Bank.

Answer Bank

70	65	0	87
31	40	38	72
9	71	66	11
33	2	15	20
47	19	6	13
55	27	39	52
24	46		

1. California + North Carolina = _____

2. Florida – South Carolina = _____

3. Utah + Colorado + Arizona + New Mexico = _____

4. Ohio – Vermont – Maine = _____

5. North Dakota x South Dakota = _____

6. Georgia ÷ Kentucky = _____

7. Pennsylvania – Illinois = _____

8. New York – New Jersey = _____

9. Oklahoma + Idaho = _____

10. Oregon – Nebraska = _____

Inauguration Day

Standards

☑ Students know what political leaders do and why leadership is necessary in a democracy.

☑ Students will analyze fiction and nonfiction texts and synthesize the information in a variety of ways.

Paired Texts Reading and Activities

★ **Taking the Oath** (pages 109–110)—Have students read the reader's theater script independently. Then, assign roles to student volunteers and have them perform the reader's theater in front of the class. Ask students why they think we have a president and why it is important that our country has a leader. Discuss this as a class. Read the presidential oath on page 110 to students. Ask them if they think this simple oath is appropriate for such an important job. Instruct students to complete page 110 individually or in pairs. Ask for volunteers to share their answers.

★ **Becoming the President** (page 111)—Read the informational text on page 111 as a class. Instruct students to number the different events that take place on Inauguration Day. Create a timeline of events on the board with students. Ask students which Inauguration Day events they would attend if they could. Have students write paragraphs explaining why they chose those particular events.

★ **A Grand Event** (page 112)—In this activity, students will use information from both the informational text and the reader's theater to complete the graphic organizer. Have them complete the page individually or in pairs. When students have finished, ask them to share their responses with other students.

★ **My Idea of Grand** (page 113)—With this activity, students list ideas on how they would make the next presidential inauguration a grand affair that people would remember for years to come. When students have finished this activity, have them share their best ideas and drawings with the class.

Inauguration Day *(cont.)*

Primary Source Connection

★ **Protecting the President Primary Source**
(pages 114–115)—Study the primary source and read the background information on page 114 with students. Then, go over the directions on page 115 as a class. Instruct students to answer the questions on page 115 individually. When students have finished, have them share their answers with partners.

Puzzle Time!

★ **Missing Word Vocabulary Puzzle** (page 116)—Students will enjoy using the pictures and sentence clues to help them find the missing vocabulary words.

★ **Riddle Me This Inauguration Puzzle** (page 117)—Students will have fun trying to solve the riddle by deciding if the statements about Inauguration Day are true or false. If they choose correctly, the answers will solve the riddle!

Answer Key

A Grand Event (page 112)

Possible answers include:

Question: Do you think Inauguration Day is an important and grand event?		
What I Already Know About the Topic	**Support from Fiction and Nonfiction Texts**	**My Answer to the Question**
When a new president takes office, it is a big day. It is exciting to see the new president. It is fun to see the speeches and parades.	Fiction text: The president-elect is nervous. If it weren't a big event, he would not be nervous. Nonfiction text: there are lots of TV cameras and reporters; there is a parade and crowds of people; there are balls	Answers may vary based on columns 1 and 2.

Protecting the President Primary Source
(pages 114–115)

Students' pictures will vary but may include: increased police presence in the area; safety glass around the podium; cameras; metal detectors

Missing Word Vocabulary Puzzle (page 116)
1. oath
2. inaugural address
3. balls
4. Inauguration

Challenge: Sentences and drawing may vary but should be based on information provided in the passages.

Riddle Me This Inauguration Day Puzzle (page 117)
1. J (true) 5. Q (false) 9. C (true)
2. O (false) 6. U (true) 10. Y (true)
3. H (true) 7. I (false)
4. N (false) 8. N (false)

Riddle Answer: **John Quincy** Adams

★ ★ ★ Taking the Oath ★ ★ ★

President Jackson: Are you sure you want to walk to the Capitol building? We could take the car.

President-elect: I would prefer to walk, Mr. President, if you don't mind.

President Jackson: You are aware that it is freezing outside? It may even begin to snow soon.

President-elect: That is fine. I have a warm coat. I am just very nervous. I think the walk and the fresh air will help calm my nerves. Are all presidents-elect this nervous before they take the oath?

President Jackson: (*laughs*) I would imagine so. Well, I can't imagine Teddy Roosevelt being nervous. He may be the exception to the rule.

President-elect: (*laughs*) I agree. I am afraid I did not get much sleep last night. I kept having nightmares about flubbing the oath.

President Jackson: The oath? But that is the easy part! It's short and simple. I was more nervous about giving my inauguration speech.

President-elect: Don't get me wrong. I am nervous about that, as well. But I do feel my speech is strong and will connect with both my supporters and those who did not vote for me.

President Jackson: I am sure your speech will be excellent. Should we start walking? You do not want to be late for your own inauguration.

President-elect: Yes. Let's get started on our way. After the oath and the speeches, how will the rest of the day fare? Is there anything else I should be nervous about?

President Jackson: Not at all. But you did see the schedule. It is a long day and night. The only thing you should be nervous about is passing out from exhaustion.

President-elect: I'm quite excited for the parade and balls. I want to shake the hands of my supporters as I walk along the parade route. But I am definitely most excited to begin my work as the next president of the United States. I know I can make a difference in our nation. I know I can improve it and help those in need.

President Jackson: I believe in you and so do the citizens of this country. After all, they chose *you* to lead them. I know you will accomplish a great many things during your presidency.

President-elect: Thank you, Mr. President. Your kind words and support mean the world to me. I believe all butterflies have left my stomach. I'm ready to take that oath!

★ ★ ★ **Taking the Oath** *(cont.)* ★ ★ ★

Directions: The following is the oath of office taken by the president of the United States. Read the oath. Then, answer the questions below.

> I do solemnly swear (or affirm) that I will faithfully execute the Office of President of the United States, and will to the best of my Ability, preserve, protect, and defend the Constitution of the United States.

1. What is the president promising to do in the oath? Explain it in your own words.

    _____

    _____

    _____

2. Is this what you expected the oath to be? Why or why not?

    _____

    _____

    _____

3. How would you change the oath? Write your suggested oath below.

    _____

    _____

    _____

    _____

★ ★ ★ Becoming the President ★ ★ ★

Inauguration Day is on January 20. It takes place in the year after the election. *Inauguration* means "a ceremonial induction into office." Inauguration Day marks the end of one presidential term and the beginning of another. It is a time of celebration. There is a parade. There are many fancy balls. It is a long day. But it is also a very exciting one. There are TV cameras and reporters. Many people come out to see the festivities. Even more people watch it on TV.

Inauguration Day begins in the morning. The current president meets with the president-elect. The two travel to the Capitol building together. This is where the new president is sworn in. The vice president is sworn in, too. This means they take their oaths of office. They promise to do the best they can. They pledge to defend the Constitution. The chief justice of the United States Supreme Court leads the president in the oath.

There is music and singing. Prayers are often said, and poetry is read. Many speeches are given. The most important speech is the new president's speech. It is known as

the Inaugural Address. In the speech, the president explains his or her plan for the future of the country. President Kennedy gave one of the most famous inaugural addresses. In it he stated, "Ask not what your country can do for you—ask what you can do for your country."

In the afternoon, there is a parade for the president. The president walks or rides in a car down Pennsylvania Avenue to the White House. President Harding was the first president to travel this route in a car. Crowds of people line the parade route hoping to catch a glimpse of the new president.

The evening is filled with fancy inaugural balls. People buy tickets to these balls. They hope to meet and celebrate with the new president. The president travels from ball to ball. President and Mrs. Clinton went to 14 balls on the night of his inauguration!

Inauguration Day is a grand event. It helps Americans remember how important the presidency is. It reminds them that our country is a democracy. We get to choose our leaders.

Directions: If you could attend one of the events that occur on Inauguration Day, which one would you choose? Why? Explain your answer in a paragraph and then draw a picture of you at the event.

Name _____ Date _____

★ ★ ★ A Grand Event ★ ★ ★

Directions: Use both texts to complete the graphic organizer below.

Question: In what ways is Inauguration Day an important and grand event?		
What I Already Know About the Topic	**Support from Nonfiction and Fiction Texts**	**My Answer to the Question**

★ ★ ★ My Idea of Grand ★ ★ ★

Directions: Imagine you have been asked to plan the next presidential Inauguration Day. What would you do to make it a grand historical event? How would you make it an inauguration that people would remember for years to come? Write your ideas on the lines below. Then, draw scenes from the day in the boxes at the bottom of the page.

_____

_____

_____

_____

_____

★ ★ ★ Protecting the President Primary Source ★ ★ ★

Primary Source Background Information

When a president wins a second term, there is still an inauguration. Abraham Lincoln won a second term as president in 1864. The Civil War was coming to an end. The South was facing certain defeat. Many Southerners were not happy with President Lincoln. Lincoln's security team was worried that someone would try to take the life of the president. So they kept careful watch over the president that day.

This picture shows Lincoln giving his Inaugural Address. In his speech, he spoke about the meaning of the Civil War. He reminded people that the war was fought to end slavery. He wanted people to move forward and treat one another with compassion. There are many people listening to the president's speech. One of those people was John Wilkes Booth. A little over a month later, Booth would assassinate the president.

Alexander Gardner, Library of Congress

★ ★ Protecting the President Primary Source (cont.) ★ ★

Directions: Being president is hard and sometimes dangerous work. A team called the Secret Service helps to keep the president safe. Pretend you are a member of the Secret Service team. Fill in the graphic organizer. What advice would you give the president on staying safe? How would you help to keep the president safe? Why is it important to keep the president safe? Write or draw your answers in the boxes below.

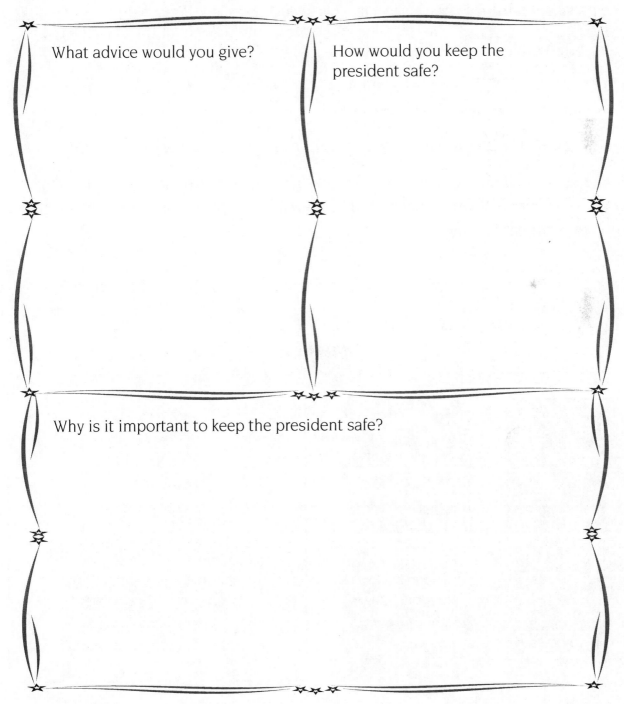

What advice would you give?

How would you keep the president safe?

Why is it important to keep the president safe?

★ ★ ★ Missing Word Vocabulary Puzzle ★ ★ ★

Directions: Read each sentence about inaugurations. Try to fill in the missing vocabulary word. The pictures at the bottom of the page are clues!

1. The president and vice president must take an _____ . They promise to do the best job that they can.

2. The president must also give a speech. This speech is called the _____ _____ . In this speech the president talks about the plans he or she has for the country.

3. After the president's parade, the evening is filled with many fancy _____. There will be lots of dancing at these parties.

4. All these celebrations take place on _____ Day.

Challenge: Write your own missing word sentence about inaugurations. Remember to give clues in the sentence that will help a person figure out the missing word. Also, draw a clue for the word in the space provided.

_____

_____

_____

1.

2.

3.

4.

Challenge

★ ★ ★ Riddle Me This Inauguration Day Puzzle ★ ★ ★

Directions: Many things happen on Inauguration Day. Read the statements below. Choose if they are true or false by circling the correct letter. Then, write the letters you circled in order at the bottom of the page to solve the riddle.

	True	False
1. On this day, the new vice president takes an oath of office.	J	F
2. On this day, the new president must pass a new law.	R	O
3. On this day, the new president gives an address.	H	D
4. On this day, only Congress hears the new president's speech.	D	N
5. On this day, the new president attends one ball in the afternoon.	K	Q
6. On this day, people line the streets to watch the parade.	U	E
7. On this day, the weather is usually hot because it is summer.	R	I
8. On this day, the new president votes.	C	N
9. On this day, many cameras and news reporters cover the events.	C	H
10. On this day, there is a lot of celebrating.	Y	N

I refused to show up at Andrew Jackson's inauguration because I was mad that I lost the election to him! Who am I?

___ ___ ___ ___   ___ ___ ___ ___ ___ ___   **Adams**

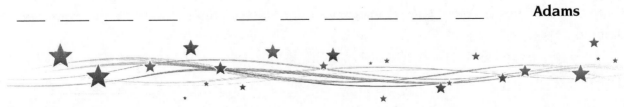

★ ★ ★ Culminating Activity—Mock Election ★ ★ ★

Students have learned the various steps in the election process. Now, give students a chance to participate in a mock election! Follow the steps below.

Materials
★ **copies of** *Voter Registration Form* and *Presidential Election Ballot* (page 120)   ★ **ballot box**
★ **art supplies**   ★ **patriotic decorations, music, snacks** (*optional*)
★ **student sign-in sheet**

Step 1—Getting to Know the Candidates

Tell students there will be a mock presidential election! Two candidates will be running in the election: Candidate A and Candidate B. (**Note**: You can use the fake candidates below or the real candidates in the current election.) Recreate the table below on the board. Go over each candidate with the students. Tell students to take their time and really think about which candidate will make the best leader for the country.

Candidate A's Traits and Platform	Candidate B's Traits and Platform
worked as a teacher for 20 years	comes from a long line of politicians
currently a senator	father was a vice president
believes in personal responsibility	member of the House of Representatives
began a privately run, community organization to keep forests clean	helped pass anti-pollution laws
is careful spending tax dollars	believes in spending tax dollars to help people
believes government should be run by the people	believes the government should provide health care for its citizens
intelligent and a quick thinker	can be shy and quiet but gets along well with others
confident	makes quick decisions, seeming selfish at times
has been caught in a few small lies	is hard working but stern
tends to change opinions on topics often	

Step 2—Register to Vote

Distribute copies of the *Voter Registration Form* (page 120). Have students complete the forms and turn them in to you.

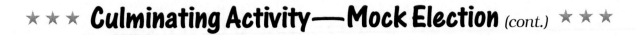

★ ★ ★ Culminating Activity—Mock Election *(cont.)* ★ ★ ★

Step 3—Campaigning

Have students make campaign posters, buttons, and slogans for the candidates they support. Place these items around the classroom. Ask students to come to the front of the class and give speeches trying to convince others to vote for their candidate. **Note**: Tell students they can change their mind about the candidate they support anytime during the election. They do not have to make a final decision until voting time.

Step 4—Voting

Before class begins, set up two private voting areas (booths) and have a ballot box ready. Have a list of student names written vertically on a sheet of paper, ready for students to sign in as they vote. Also have copies of the *Presidential Election Ballot* (page 120) ready. When students arrive, review the platforms of each candidate. Provide students with five minutes of silence to think about who they will be voting for. Randomly divide the class into four groups or "states." Explain that State A will be the largest and have 7 electoral votes. State B will be smaller and have 5 electoral votes. State C will have 3 electoral votes. State D will have 2 electoral votes. Next, call students up in pairs from their electoral state to cast their votes. Have them sign in on the student sign-in sheet and give each student a ballot. After all students have voted, "close" the polls.

Step 5—Counting the Votes

Recreate the Election Results tables on the board. Review the concepts of *popular* and *electoral* votes. As you take each ballot out of the box, add a tally mark to the chart in the appropriate place on the table. Encourage students to cheer when their candidates receive votes. After all the popular votes have been counted, count the electoral votes. Determine the winner. If time permits, have an inaugural celebration with decorations, patriotic songs, and yummy snacks.

Election Results

	Popular Votes Received for Candidate A	Popular Votes Received for Candidate B
State A		
State B		
State C		
State D		
Total		

	Possible Electoral Votes	Candidate A's Electoral Votes	Candidate B's Electoral Votes
State A	7		
State B	5		
State C	3		
State D	2		
Total			

★ ★ ★ Culminating Activity—Mock Election (cont.) ★ ★ ★

Voter Registration Form

1 Last Name	2 ☐ Male ☐ Female

3 First Name	4 Middle Name

5 Address	6 Phone Number

7 Email (optional)	8 Date of Birth (MM/DD/YYYY)

9 Are you a United States citizen? ☐ Yes ☐ No	10 Are you 18 years or older? ☐ Yes ☐ No

11 To which party do you belong?	FOR OFFICIAL USE ONLY

Presidential Election Ballot

Place an X in the box in front of the ONE candidate for whom you are voting. Fold the ballot and place it in the ballot box.

☐ Candidate A

☐ Candidate B

☐ Write-in Candidate: _____